THE UNION STAR

BROOKNEAL, VIRGINIA OBITUARIES

1916-1920

compiled by
Cynthia Farris Utterback

HERITAGE BOOKS
2006

HERITAGE BOOKS

AN IMPRINT OF HERITAGE BOOKS, INC.

Books, CDs, and more—Worldwide

For our listing of thousands of titles see our website
at
www.HeritageBooks.com

Published 2006 by
HERITAGE BOOKS, INC.
Publishing Division
65 East Main Street
Westminster, Maryland 21157-5026

International Standard Book Number: 978-0-7884-4116-7

I dedicate this book to Cora Stafford Daniel Kreger, my grandmother, who inspired the love and passion in me for family history. Cindy Utterback

I would like to thank Wilma Dotson, who gave me the confidence that this work could be done and my husband, Jeff, who has endured my many long hours at the library and the computer.

Foreword

Brookneal is located at the southeastern end of Campbell County, Virginia, which borders on the Halifax, Pittsylvania, Appomattox and Charlotte County lines. Brookneal is thirty miles south of Lynchburg. In the 2000 census, there were 1,259 residents in Brookneal.

The town of Brookneal was established in 1802 from the lands of John Brooke and his wife, Sarah Neal.

The Union Star was established in 1906 by the Ginther family, reporting news from Brookneal and Halifax, Charlotte, and Pittsylvania Counties.

Today, *The Union Star* is located on Main Street in Brookneal and is published once a week with news and community events.

January 7, 1916

Mr. Hugh Elliott, who died in Richmond, January 1, where he had been taken for medical treatment, was buried in the Hat Creek cemetery at 2 o'clock. Had he lived until the 18th of February he would have been seventy years old.

Mr. Elliott leaves a widow, who was Miss Josephine Holt; three daughters, Mrs. R. H. Waddell, of Bedford City, and Mrs. J. C. Brown, of Newbern, N. C., and little Miss Frances Elliott, of Hat Creek and two sons, Messrs. O. C. Elliott, of Richmond, and W. S. Elliott, of Greenville, N.C.

Services were conducted by Revs. W. S. Royal, John B. Williams and G. A. Chocklett

January 14, 1916

NOTICE-On Friday, Jan.21st, 1916, I will offer for sale at public auction to the highest bidder all of the personal property of the late H. N. Elliott, deceased, consisting of household and kitchen furniture, plantation tools of every description, one 2-horse wagon and harness, one carriage, one buggy and harness, one-half interest in a Deering binder, one horse, two head of cattle, about fifty bushels of wheat, about forty bushels of corn and many other things.

Sale to commence promptly at 10 o'clock.

Terms made known on day of sale.

Wirt Williams, Administrator.

January 28, 1916

Wm. S. Rasnick died at his home in Dickenson county, Va., on the 15th of this month. He was a victim of dropsy. Mr. Rasnick was in his sixtieth year, and is survived by seven daughters, two sons, six brothers, and one sister. He was a member of Dyer Lodge No.240, I.O.O.F., Nora, Va., and was also a prominent and very active member of Local Dante Socialist Party, being one of the charter members and candidate for supervisor in Ervington District on that ticket in 1915. Mr. Rasnick had a wide acquaintance and was well liked by all. He will be sadly missed in the community.

February 4, 1916

Mrs. Martha J. Harvey, who had been an invalid for several years, died at the home of her daughter, Mrs. John E. Wood, in South Boston last Tuesday morning, age 76 years. Mrs. Harvey was the widow of the late Cole Harvey and was for many years a resident of Brookneal where she is remembered by our older citizens.

James M. Lawson, a former resident of Brookneal, died at the home of his son-in-law, S. D. Umstead in Lynchburg Saturday morning January 29th, after a week's illness from grip, aged 69 years.

Mr. Lawson was a native of Campbell county and had represented this county for two terms in the Virginia House of Delegates.

He was for several years a prominent and progressive citizen of Brookneal and took an active interest in all things that pertained to the building up of the town. He built and conducted the hotel now managed by Mrs. L. D. Harvey, and also owned a block of stores on the site now occupied by the Williams drug store, postoffice and bank, besides having other business interests. He was postmaster during the last Cleveland administration.

His remains were brought to Brookneal Saturday evening and on Sunday taken to Hat Creek and interred in the family graveyard, the burial service being conducted by W. C. Walker in the absence of any available minister.

Mr. Lawson's wife died about two months ago. He is survived by three daughters, Mrs. W. H. Barnes, of Christiansburg; Mrs. W. A. Rice, of Brookneal, and Mrs. S. D. Umstead, of Lynchburg.

February 11, 1916

The remains of Mr. Pub Clark was brought here Sunday night from Williamsburg where he had been for several years for treatment. He was buried at his fathers old home near Hat Creek. The burial services were conducted by Rev. W. Y. Scales.

February 18, 1916

Misses Jewell and Arye Holt attended the funeral of their cousin, Miss Lizzie Cothran, at Edge Hill church last Sunday.

February 25, 1916

On the morning of January 4th, 1916, the death angel visited the home of Mr. W. L. Taylor and took from him his beloved wife, Rosa Lee, aged 31 years.
She was a devoted wife and mother, and a friend to all who knew her. Her remains were laid to rest in Oak Grove cemetery. The burial services were conducted by Rev. W. L. Mays. She leaves her mother, husband, five children, four brothers, two sisters, and a host of friends and relatives to mourn her loss.
But the loved ones grieve not for her. She is not dead but sleeping. There she will be waiting for us on that peaceful shore where suffering and sorrow are never known.
Dear Rosa, thou hast gone but not forgotten;
Sweet memory of thee will never die.
We loved the well but Jesus loved thee best,
So he has taken thee home to rest.
We have read that the Heavenly Shepherd
Oft gathers safe into his fold
Our loved ones by taking them from us,
In his arms from the suffering and cold.
God has taken our loved one, our Rosa,
To his home in Heaven above,
That our hearts may some day answer
To the dear, sweet call of his love.
Thy way, it is best, our Father,
Submissive we bow to thy will,
But thy hand lay on our crushed spirits
And say to our hearts "Be still."
By her little cousin, Mary G. Rudder

Miss Mary Elizabeth Cothran, familiarly known as "Lizzie," died at 6:15 am Feb. 12, 1916, at the home of her parents at Edge following an illness of three weeks. She was 16 years and 7 months old and had been a consistent member of Edge Baptist church about three and a half years. Her parents, Mr. and Mrs. E. H. Cothran, five brothers, Samuel B., John B., Frank, Joe and Jesse and one little sister, Bertha, survive her. Her remains were laid to rest beside a sister and two brothers who had preceeded her to the grave, in the cemetery at Edge Bill (Hill) Baptist church, near Level Run in Pittsylvania county, Sunday afternoon. Funeral services conducted by her pastor, Rev. J. A. Barnhardt.

Mr. and Mrs. E. H. Henderson, of Roanoke, spent the weekend with the latter's parents, Mr. and Mrs. J. O. Terry. They were suddenly called to the home of Mr. Henderson's father, who died Thursday morning.

March 3, 1916

George E. Pulley, for the past ten years agent for the Norfolk & Western Railway at Clarkton, died Monday night from a hemorrhage after an illness of several days, aged 40 years. He is survived by his wife, who was formerly Miss Alice Marshall and three children. His remains were taken to Woodsdale, N.C., Wednesday for burial.

The neighborhood of Seneca was saddened by the news of the sudden death of Mrs. J. B. Poindexter which occurred at her home at that place early last Sunday morning, caused by heart failure. Mrs. Poindexter was 54 years of age and is survived by her husband and six children, the daughters being Mrs. L. M. Ware, of Seneca, Mrs. S. F. Armstrong, of Nashville, Tenn., and Miss Harriette Poindexter, of Seneca. The sons are Messrs. J. R., Tucker and Herbert Poindexter. Besides her immediate family, Mrs. Poindexter is survived by one sister, Mrs. M. H. Harris, of Gladys, Va., and four brothers, Messrs. W. E and E. W. Walthall, of Gladys, R. O. Walthall of Seneca, and N. I. Walthall, of Brookneal. Mrs. Poindexter had been a member of the Methodist church from early childhood, and had always lead an earnest Christian life. She was dearly beloved by all who knew her and will be greatly missed. Interment took place Tuesday, February 29th, in the family burying ground at Seneca.

N. I. Walthall was called to Seneca Sunday by the death of his sister, Mrs. Mattie Poindexter.

March 10, 1916

Constable S. C. Henderson has purchased the farm of the late Thomas Dyer, and will move into it in the spring. The farm consists of about 163 acres.

March 17, 1916

Francis Alexander Scott, a well known citizen of Halifax county, died at his home at 1:30 o'clock Monday afternoon, March 13, after an illness of three months from a complication of diseases, aged 61 years.

Deceased was a son of the late Patrick H. Scott and was born and reared at "Seven Islands," on the border of Halifax county. He was the eldest of a family of four brothers and two sisters and his death was the first break in the family circle. He never enjoyed robust health, having suffered from a long illness when a youth from typhoid fever which weakened his system, but being possessed of a cheerful and sanguine temperament he was never known to utter a complaint, whatever the state of his health, the weather or other conditions. For many years he had been a member of the Brookneal Presbyterian church.

All that loving hearts could suggest or willing hands perform was done for his comfort in his last days. He was conscious of his approaching end and was resigned to his fate, dying at peace with the world and in full hope of salvation.

In December 1877, he married Miss Mary C. Pleasants. Of this union nine children were born, all of whom are living. He is survived by his wife and the following children: Mrs. J. C. Arendall, of Nathalie; Mrs. Henry S. Ross, of Newport News; Misses Annie, Clara, Georgia and Frankie Scott; John R. Scott, of Dayton, Ohio; Patrick H. Scott, of Jacksonville, Fla., and Charles A. Scott, of William and Mary College. Also, the following brothers and sisters: C. C., W. B., and C. Y. Scott and Mrs. R. R. Todd, all of this vicinity, and Mrs. S. B. Yuille, of Norfolk.

After appropriate funeral services conducted at the home Tuesday afternoon by Rev. G. W. Ribble, of Houston, the remains were interred in the family plot, the following acting as pallbearers: R. F. Connally, C. S. Stephens, Bezer Snell, W. R. Walker, John T. Adams and Dr. W. O. Tune. The flower bearers were: E. R. Monroe, P. P. Smith, W. C. Walker and R. L. Burton. Many friends attended the obsequies as a mark of respect to his memory and many floral tributes were sent by sorrowing friends. The announcement of Mr. Scott's death will be received with profound sorrow throughout this entire section and the sympathies of all go out to the bereaved family.

March 24, 1916

Mr. Charles W. Myers died at his home at Cedar Forest, Halifax county, Thursday, March 16th, at one o'clock, of heart trouble. Mr. Myers was in his sixty-ninth year. Interment took place on Friday in the family burying ground. Mr. Myers is survived by his widow and nine sons, T. O. and M. D., of Brookneal; W. P., of Harlan, Ky., G. A. and C. R., of Danville; J. B. and C. I., of Charlotte, N.C.; J. W., of Clarkton, and S. R., who resided at home; also two daughters, Mrs. J. T. Wilborn, of Cedar Forest, and Mrs. G. H. Franklin, of Pittsville. Mr. Myers was a native of Pittsylvania county. He was a veteran of the civil war and had resided at Cedar Forest for thirty years. He was a member of Clover Bottom Baptist church. The funeral services were conducted by Rev. Barbour, of Brights.

Death of Little Child-On the 14th day of March the death angel visited the home of Mr. and Mrs. W. E. Roakes, near Gladys, and took away their baby daughter, Lotty, aged seven months and four days. The little body was laid to rest at Wesleyberry, by the side of her three little brothers that had gone before. She was sick only a few days. The bereaved parents have the sympathy of the entire community.

March 31, 1916

Mrs. Hannah Alice Klein, died at her home near Gladys, on March 16, age 53 years, eleven months and 3 days. She was a native of Ohio, and a member of the Lutheran church. Mrs. Klein, before her marriage, was a Miss Hoy, and was married December 9th, 1894, and moved to Campbell county, Va., with her family, several years ago, where she, by her lovable disposition and beautiful Christian character, had made a host of friends. She was highly esteemed in the community in which she lived.

She leaves her husband and three sons, Karl of Ohio, Frank and Jacob, of Campbell county, Va., to mourn their loss.

There being no minister in the community at the time of her death, at the request of her husband, J. B. Connelly, one of their neighbors, held a brief service in their home after which her body was taken to McClure, Ohio, for burial.

Much sympathy is felt for her family. Mr. Klein asked the writer to say that he could not find words to express his gratitude to his neighbors for their kindness during the illness of his companion and at the time of her death.

April 21, 1916

Tuesday night, April 18, R. H. Stephens died at the home of his son-in-law, P. P. Smith, at the age of 84 years. Mr. Stephens had been in failing health for some time and his death was not unexpected. He was a native of Halifax county and served in the civil war, locating at Brookneal soon after the close of war. For about forty years he conducted a wheelwright shop here. Soon after coming to Brookneal he was married to Miss Ann Smith, a daughter of Rev. John Smith. Mrs. Stephens preceded her husband to the grave about four years ago. Mr. Stephens is survived by two daughters, Mrs. P. P. Smith and Mrs. P. L. Elder, and one son, Sam Stephens, all of Brookneal. He was Justice of the Peace at Brookneal for about twenty-five years until failing health due to the infimities of age forced him to give up the office. Interment took place on Wednesday afternoon in the old Smith burying ground about two miles from Brookneal.

Mrs. Nannie Blanche Jordan, wife of W. T. Jordan, died at her home near Tola, Charlotte county, April 14th, and was buried at Midway Baptist church April 15th, the funeral service being conducted by her pastor, Rev. G. A. Chocklett, assisted by Rev. F. G. Cabaniss.

Besides her husband she leaves six children, four boys and two

7

girls, and one brother, W. J. Sublett. She had been ill about two months. She was a faithful Christian, having united with the Baptist church in early life and was tireless in her work for the Lord and showed her faith by her works, and, like Dorcas, many can testify of her good deeds to the needy, the sick and afflicted, or those who were bowed in sorrow, or needed sympathy or someone to point them to the way of life eternal. She used every opportunity to do her Master's work.

Her family will miss her but her church and community will miss her more. She was a tireless worker in the Woman's Missionary Society, of which she was president, and gave of her means for foreign and State missions, and showed her interest in State and home missions by her work among the unsaved of her community. Her heart was on fire for the salvation of men and women, whether at home or abroad. She was a faithful and most efficient Sunday school teacher and worker and many souls did she lead to her Saviour who was so precious to her. She suffered and sacrificed that she might glorify her Master, and that her life might be an example for others to follow.

She was permitted by a kind Providence to live to see all her children Christians. She was a loving, kind and true wife and mother, a kind neighbor and a true friend. She bore her suffering with patience and fell asleep rejoicing in a complete salvation, for her life was a finished product of the grace of God. We miss her, but our loss is her gain, for she has entered into her rest and reward and we can say,

"Then let us work and watch and pray,
Relying on the love
Of Him who now prepares a place
For us in Heaven above."
A Friend

May 5, 1916

Rev. J. B. Williams, Mr. and Mrs. M. L. Booth and Mrs. Worsham attended the funeral services of Mr. Henry Coates near Nathalie Monday.

May 12, 1916

Mrs. M. J. Wickliffe, oldest resident of the village will celebrate her seventieth birthday next Thursday, the 18th, and will appreciate the receipt of souvenir cards from any of her friends on that occasion. Mrs. Wickliffe has lived here the past forty years and has witnessed the erection of every house in town except seven.

Mrs. Virginia Shelton, mother of W. J. Shelton, who lives near Hat Creek, died at Durham, N.C., May 1st, aged 77 years.

C. E. Crank, of Halifax county, a member of the bridge force on the Virginian railway, fell off the pier and was drowned in Norfolk Wednesday. His body will be brought to Halifax for burial.

May 19, 1916

Quite a number of Brookneal people attended the burial service of Mr. Edgar Henderson, at Nathalie Monday.

Grace the little daughter of Cabell McDowell, died last week with whooping cough and was buried at Falling church.

On last Saturday at twelve-thirty o'clock, E. H. Henderson, a N.& W. brakeman was caught between shifting cars at Blue Ridge, and badly mashed. He was immediately taken to a Roanoke hospital where he died at seven-thirty o'clock, remaining conscious to the last. Mr. Henderson was the son of J. H. Henderson of Natalie, and lived in Brookneal about two years during the Wickliffe boom. About four years ago he married, Susie, daughter of Mr. and Mrs. J. O. Terry, of this place, who with two children, both boys, survive him.
The body was taken to Nathalie Sunday afternoon for burial, accompanied by Will Lacks and wife, Mr. and Mrs. Guy Lacks, Mr. and Mrs. Jim Spencer, and Messrs. Jones, Willard, Sherall and Flag, who were placed in charge of the remains by the railway brotherhood to which Mr. Henderson belonged. Also, J. O. Terry and Mr. Frank Henderson, of this place, who motored to Roanoke Saturday evening upon hearing of the accident, accompanied the

remains to Nathalie. The funeral service was held at Nathalie and the remains laid to rest in the Catawba cemetery. The flower bearers were Misses Mary and Jessie Carr, Miss Spencer and Mrs. Lou A. Terry.

The accident supposed to have been caused by the failure of the air brakes to work on two cars loaded with stone.

May 26, 1916

Mrs. Isabel Cooke, a charming widow of Philadelphia, and her three lovely children arrived in town last Saturday, and will be the house guests of Miss Clara Scott, at her home, Seven Islands. Mrs. Cooke will be remembered as the young and attractive bride of Mr. St. George H. Cooke. Mr. Cooke was one of the resident engineers here during the construction of the Virginia Railway, and was greatly loved and admired by all who met him. The news of his death over a year ago was received by his friends with many expressions of regret.

Prominent Brookneal Citizen Passes Away After a Short Illness-Mr. C. E. Shackleton, a well known citizen of Brookneal, died early Thursday morning after a brief illness. Mr. Shackleton had been suffering from a nervous breakdown and later developed paralysis. Mr. Shackleton was 34 years of age and had been a resident of Brookneal for about ten years, and was engaged in the mercantile business. Interment took place Saturday evening about five o'clock.

In 1912 Mr. Shackleton was married to Miss Willie Holt, of Altavista, who with one child, C. E. Junior, survives him. Mr. Shackleton is also survived by his mother, Mrs. M. A. Shackleton, who resides at Meherrin; three sisters, Mrs. L. S. Torpley, of Memphis, Tenn., Mrs. F. W. Bridgeforth, of Kenbridge and Mrs. George Redd, Jr., of Meherrin, and four brothers, A. B., of Victoria, J. S., of Meherrin, O. S., of Petersburg, and W. B., of Charlotte, N.C.

The funeral services were conducted at the grave by Rev. W. Y. Scales assisted by Rev. B. F. Bedinger, after which the remains were laid to rest in the family section of the Brookneal cemetery, in the presence of a very large gathering of friends. The grave was heaped with many beautiful floral offerings, a tribute to the esteem in which the deceased had been held by a large host of friends. Mr. Shackleton was posessed of a very sympathetic temperament and many acts of generosity unknown to the general public are entered to his credit. He will be greatly missed.

The pall bearers were, honorary: P. P. Smith, Jere White, R. A. Guthrie, W. A. Price, Dr. Tune, J. E. Webb, W. L. Proctor, N. I. Walthall, R. E. Gilliam, and S. M. Clay; Active: Frank Guthrie, J. H. Foster, W. A. Mays, E. L. Ridgeway, W. R. Walker, and C. S. Stephens. The flower bearers were: Hubert Walthall, Harold Thornton, Chas. Holt, Conway Guthrie, A. T. Canada, W. W. Rudder, C. E. Ellington and T. O. Myers.

Card of Thanks-We want to thank each and every one of our friends for their loving sympathy and kindness during the illness and hour of grief, when God saw fit to take our darling husband and brother. We thank you for the lovely flowers. It is so hard to give up our loved one, but God knew best and if we will only trust Him, He will sustain us in this hour of sorrow.

Mrs. C. E. Shackleton
His Family
Her Family

Death of Colored Woman-"Tommy," wife of Henry Randolph colored, died at Cakewalk Friday and was buried in the colored cemetery Saturday. She was about forty-five years of age.

June 2, 1916

David T. Duff, a reader of the Union Star, died at his home near Abington, Va., on Saturday night, May 25.

Mr. Duff was one of those great souls who never surpress their opinions for the sake of popularity or business advantage. He was a man of rare intellect and a keen student and analyst. His love and commiseration for his fellow man extended to the whole world and to do good was his only religion.

If the majority of mortals measured up to the moral and ethical standards held by him this old world would be a paradise instead of a seething hell of poverty and despair. May his kind increase.

The remains of Mr. Alexander Asher, age 55 years, who died

Friday last at Staunton were brought here and buried Monday at Falling River church, the services being conducted by Rev. W. S. Royal.

Mr. Asher is survived by his widow and several children, who reside about three miles from this place.

Lizzie O. Fore, who was 88 years old, died suddenly on Saturday at her home in Gladys. She was a member of a prominent Campbell county family, but the only surviving member now is a daughter, Mrs. William Whately, of Kew.

June 9, 1916

Mrs. J. Hendricks was laid to rest in the old Sharon cemetery, Sunday afternoon. There were many friends and relatives present.

Card Of Thanks-It being impossible for us to see each one personally or reach them all by letter, we take this method of expressing our heartfelt thanks to the many good friends who so kindly tendered the use of their automobiles and presented so many beautiful floral offerings and otherwise displayed their friendship and sympathy at the death and burial of our beloved sister, Mrs. V. H. Lawson.
The Family

Prominent Brookneal Lady passes to Great Beyond-Mrs. Victoria Harvey Lawson died Friday June 2, at the Home and Retreat hospital in Lynchburg, after an illness of about two months. Mrs. Lawson was fifty-six years of age. The remains were brought to Brookneal where the funeral services were conducted in the Baptist church by Rev. W. S. Royall, after which she was taken to Roanoke church in Charlotte county for interment beside the body of her husband who died about eighteen years ago.
Soon after the death of her husband Mrs. Lawson came to Brookneal where she made her home for the remainder of her life. She had been a member of the Baptist church since early childhood and had ever been a consistent Christian and earnest, faithful worker. She was of a very sympathetic nature, always kind, helpful and considerate of others, and enjoyed a large circle of friends. She taught school a great deal and always enjoyed the

confidence and esteem of her pupils. She is survived by three brothers and three sisters: Henry W. Harvey, of Phenix; C. W., of Brookneal, and W. C., of Lynchburg, and Mrs. I. M. Smith, of Lynchburg, Mrs. W. L. Williams and Mrs. R. F. Connelly, of Brookneal.

R.F.D. 2, Nathalie, Va., June 6.- Shortly after midnight last Friday morning the enemy, death, came and took from our midst, brother L. D. Martin, who had been suffering from cancer of the mouth and throat for several months, which finally reached the large artery in his neck and bled so much that he never rallied from it. He was a consistent christian and a member of the Masonic Order and also the Woodmen of the World.
The funeral service was conducted by Rev. J. H. Bass, his pastor, after which the body was turned over to the Masons for burial. The pallbearers were the nephews of the deceased, A. W. Hankley, J. J. Hankley, J. M. Hankley, R. T. Tribble, E. H. Tribble, and O. M. Tribble. The honorary pallbearers were six members of the W.O.W., S. Y. Clack, B. S. McCraw, J. W. Dunaway, G. W. Fisher, A. P. Mills and Hampton Coats, and sister, Mrs. Celia Thaxton, of this place.
The flower bearers were the nieces of the deceased, Misses Cora Hankley, Mamie Tribble, Bernice Tribble, Hallie Thaxton, Beulah Thaxton and Kate Thaxton, accompanied by F. R. Henderson, H. K. Arendall, H. C. Mills, Clarence Crews, Walter Hunt and Frank Hukson.
The deceased is survived by his wife who was Miss Nannie Tribble, and four brothers, Tom of Nathalie; Mann, of near Houston; and Charlie and John, of South Boston, and one sister, Mrs. Celia Thaxton, of this place.

June 16, 1916

On Saturday morning, June 3rd, Mrs. Martha W. Hendrick passed away to dwell with her Heavenly Father. She was 72 years of age and was a true Christian and served her Master well. Her remains were laid to rest in the cemetery at Sharon Church Sunday afternoon at 4o'clock. She was the wife of J. D. Hendrick and had been a resident of Campbell county since her marriage. She is survived by one son, J. J. Hendrick, and one daughter, Mrs. M. A.

13

Easter, both of whom live near Brookneal, also several
grandchildren are left to mourn her loss. She had made her home
with her granddaughter, Mrs. Dunaway, for a good many years.

Just a few days ago you left us;
How we miss you, mother dear;
We remember all your kindness;
As we drop a pensive tear.
Gone, dear mother, gone forever;
How we miss your loving face;
But you left us to remember
No one else can till your place.
Though you're gone you're not forgotten.
Never will your memory fade;
Loving mother, we will often
Linger round your silent grave.

June 23, 1916

Mrs. I. M. Smith, of Lynchburg, who came down to attend the
funeral of her brother, H. W. Harvey, returned home Wednesday.

Death of Little Boy-The death angel has again visited Brookneal,
this time summoning Henry Calvin, the little 23 month-old son of
Mr. and Mrs. S. T. Holt. The little fellow died Monday evening
after a short illness from whooping cough. Little Henry was the
baby in a family of eight children- six sisters and one brother
surviving him. The little body was laid to rest in the Brookneal
cemetery Tuesday evening about four o'clock, Rev. J. B. Williams
officiating. The family has the heartfelt sympathy of all our
citizens. Many beautiful floral offering were heaped upon the little
grave.
The pallbearers were, C. S. Stephens, A. T. Thornton, Louis Lash,
Frank Lash and S. A. Guthrie. The flower girls were, Hassie
Henderson, Gertrude Lash, Selma Henderson, Melba Maddox,
Beulah Worsham, Eulalia Bailey, Ruth Ellington, Dorothy and
Mabe Ridgeway, Ethel and Edna Newcombe

Henry W. Harvey died Saturday at his home near Aspen, in
Charlotte County, age 64 years. He had been ill for several
months. Interment was made in the family burying ground Sunday

afternoon, the funeral services being preached by Rev. Ryburn, of Brookneal Presbyterian church, in the presence of a large gathering of friends of the deceased. Mr. Harvey had been in former years, sheriff of Charlotte county, and was widely known and well liked by all. He was a brother of Mrs. W. L. Williams and Mrs. R. F. Connelly, of Brookneal. Other brothers and sisters are C. W. Harvey of Brookneal, and Mrs. I. M. Smith, of Lynchburg. Mr. Harvey's death, coming so soon after the death of his sister, Mrs. V. H. Lawson, is a severe blow to the family.

Card of Thanks-We desire to express our sincere thanks to the good people of Brookneal for their kindness in our time of sorrow over the loss of our little son. Especially do we wish to thank those who tendered the use of their automobiles.
S. T. Holt and family

Naruna Notes-Our neighborhood was saddened Sunday by the sudden death of Mr. Hubert Scott, who had been in failing health for several years. We extend our deepest sympathy to the bereaved family.

July 7, 1916

In Memoriam-Henry Calvin Holt, youngest child of Mr. and Mrs. S. T. Holt, departed this life Monday, June 19, 1916 aged 22 months, 19 days.
In the cold grave little Henry sleeps
While the angels are watching near;
At home his parents weep,
For they miss little Henry so dear.
Little Henry's sufferings are over.
His sweet little body is at rest.
His soul from every pain set free.
Lies silent on his Savior's breast.
We know there is room up there for all
Who only await their Savior's call
Jesus bids His loved ones come
To that dear Heavenly home.
'Tis God who rules the heavenly home.
In that fair world of eternal life:

'Tis God who calls our dear ones home.
From this world of endless strife.
Henry's angel form will longingly wait,
His face like the sun so bright,
For his parents to meet him above
In heaven where there is no night.
Ayre Holt

July 21, 1916

Killed By Train-Andrew Elder aged about 35 years and unmarried, whose home was in Charlotte county, some 8 or 10 miles from Brookneal, was killed on the Virginian Railroad about two miles east of Brookneal, between 6 o'clock Thursday evening and 9 a.m. Friday. He had been in Brookneal on Thursday and started back home that evening and it is supposed was run over by a train as his remains when found Friday morning were considerably mangled. An inquest was held over them at the Virginian depot and the verdict was in accordance with the evidence, after which the remains were turned over to his friends.

Mrs. W. F. Gilliam died at her home, near Naruna, last Tuesday night, aged 70 years. The remains were laid to rest in the family burying ground Wednesday afternoon.
Mrs. Gilliam is survived by her husband and ten children, one son, R. E., living in Brookneal. She was a native of Campbell county, and was Miss Jane Hamlet. The funeral services were conducted by her pastor, Rev. Sayers, assisted by Dr. Hamilton, of Lynchburg. A very large crowd assembled to pay their last respects to the deceased, thus attesting to the very high esteem in which she was held by all who knew her.

July 28, 1916

Card of Thanks-Mr. W. F. Gilliam and family wish to thank the attending physicians, ministers of the community and the many friends and neighbors for their kindness and attention shown his wife and their mother during her last illness and death. Their sympathy has been a balm to their broken hearts.

The funeral services of Jane Hamlet Gilliam, wife of Walter F. Gilliam, were held Wednesday afternoon, July 19, at Landover, the Gilliam homestead near Naruna, Campbell county, conducted by Dr. W. W. Hamilton, of Lynchburg, assisted by Rev. R. O. Soyars, pastor of Ebenezer Baptist church, of which the deceased was a beloved member.

The following acted as pall bearers: J. P. Pillow, T. H. Sublett, T. C. Asher, J. H. Clark, Thomas Whately, and J. C. Gilliam.

The beautiful and numerous flower offerings were carried by James R. Gilliam, Jr., Edward Gilliam Evans, Misses Gladys Gilliam, Thelma Evans, Annie and Mattie Pillow.

The singing of the hymns, "Asleep in Jesus," "Face to Face," "Beyond the Smiling and the Weeping," and "How Firm A Foundation" were sweetly rendered by Prof. J. E. Peterson, Dr. and Mrs. W. P. Williams, Mrs. W. O. Tune, Miss Katie Mason and Hubert Walthall, all of Brookneal.

The deceased is survived by her husband and the following children: A. H. Gilliam, Nichols, S.C.; Mrs. M. H. Whitlow, Brookneal, Va.; Sally V. Gilliam, Naruna, Va.; Mrs. W. J. Abbett, Randolph, Va.; W. F. Gilliam, Jr., Naruna, Va.; G. D. and J. T. Gilliam, Lynchburg, Va.; Rosa M. and Ruth J. Gilliam, Naruna, Va., all of whom were present at the funeral services.

August 4, 1916

Charles H. Foster departed this life on the 22d of June, 1916, in his 69th year. He joined Union Hill Baptist church early in life and was a loyal and faithful member, ready to do his part at all times. He was elected treasurer of the church when twenty-nine years old and faithfully filled this office until his death.

Whereas, it has pleased our Heavenly Father to remove from our midst our dear Brother Foster, we, the Union Hill Baptist church, do Resolve, 1st, That in the death of Brother Foster the Union Hill Baptist church has lost a most valuable member, the community a neighbor in whom all who knew him had the utmost confidence as a christian. But while our hearts are sad on account of his departure, we recognize our loss is his gain and we bow in humble submission to Him who doeth all things well.

Resolve, 2d, That we extend to his loved ones our deepest sympathy and commend them to our Saviour, who is the comforter of all mankind.

Resolve, 3d, That a copy of these tributes and resolutions be published, a copy to be sent to his loved ones, also to place them on our church record, as a token of respect for our dear brother, and with submissive hearts may we say:

"The Lord giveth and the Lord taketh, and blessed shall be His name."

Rev. W. P. Brooke,
N. S. Joy,
C. S. Jennings,
Committee.

Card of Thanks-We wish to thank the many friends for their kindness during the illness and death of our husband and brother. Every deed and every sympathizing word were highly appreciated when we were bowed so deep in sorrow. Thanks for the pretty flowers, which were many. His Wife, His Family.

Died, at his home near Aspen, Va., July 12, 1916, at about 4 o'clock a.m., Luke M. Trent, aged 34 years. He was the son of Stephen M. Trent, who died Jan. 2, 1912.

His death was due to that dread disease consumption. He had been sick about seven months, confined to his bed most of the time. He was a great sufferer, but bore his afflictions with Christian fortitude. All that loving hands of kind friends and physicians could do was done, but the Lord saw best to take him. He said he was going home.

"God's will be done; I am not afraid to die." He died without a groan or struggle; just fell asleep in Jesus. Besides his wife he leaves four small children, two girls and two boys, the oldest being twins, Odella and Olney, six years old. The next girl, Irene, is four years old, and the youngest, Herman, two years. The infant baby died just one month before the father. So sad, two deaths in the house in one month's time. Weep not, dear mother and wife; they are safe with Jesus awaiting your coming.

He also leaves two sisters and four brothers, as follows: Mrs. D. M. Hancock, of Red House, Miss Missouri, Stephen, Paul, Harry, and Frank Trent, all of Abell.

He was laid to rest July 13, at 3 o'clock p.m. in the cemetery at Mt. Carmel Methodist church, of which was a member in early childhood, but later he joined Midway Baptist church, to hold membership with his companion.

The funeral service was conducted in Mt. Carmel church by his pastor, Rev. G. A. Chocklett and Rev. F. G. Cabiness.

He was a kind child, brother, husband and father, and was liked by all who knew him. We shall miss him, O, we shall miss him so. We will not grieve for him as one without hope, but will think of him as

"Safe in the arms of Jesus,
Safe on his gentle breast,
There by his loved ever shadowed
Sweetly his soul shall rest."
A Loved One.

August 18, 1916

The death angel visited the home of Mr. Tom Wilbourne at Cedar Forest, on the 10th and claimed as its victim his devoted wife, Rosa Myers Wilbourne, after an illness of only a few days. All was done for her that loving hearts and willing hands could do, still they could not stay the cruel hand of death. She was a loyal christian soldier and bore her affliction without a murmur. One could see Christ in her daily walks and her life was to serve others and many deeds she did will not be soon forgotten by her many friends. She leaves to mourn her loss a husband and three daughters, one sister, Mrs. G. W. Franklin, of Pittsylvania, nine brothers, George Myers, of Danville, Peyton, of Harlen, Ky., M. D. and T. O., of Brookneal: Charlie and John of Charlotte, N.C.; Chess of Danville; Jim of Clarkton, and Rosser of Cedar Forest, also her mother, Mrs. C. W. Myers, of Cedar Forest.
Written by one who loved her.

August 25, 1916

Death of a Child-Zora Elizabeth Burton, the little iniant (infant) daughter of Mr. and Mrs. R. L. Burton, died last Saturday morning at eight o'clock and was laid to rest in the Brookneal cemetery. All was done that loving hands could do, but Jesus found fit to take

"We miss thee, little one,

19

We miss thy little face;
Our home is sad without thee,
But Heaven we hope to meet thee."
By Loving Ones.

September 1, 1916

Just as we go to press we learn of the death of Mr. W. T. Elmore at the Home and Retreat hospital at Lynchburg as the result of a fall. Mr. Elmore was about 82 years of are (age), and was well known to the citizens of Brookneal, having spent many years in the vicinity of this place. He has several children living in Lynchburg. The remains will be brought here for burial.

September 8, 1916

Death of Comrade Jenkins-The Union Star is in receipt of a letter from Strasburg, Va., announcing the death of J. Edward Jenkins, of that place, who was run over and killed in the railroad yards at Cleveland, Ohio, where he had been employed for some time. Mr. Jenkins was about 40 years of age and leaves a widow and four children. He was a charter member of Local Strasburg Socialists Party and served as secretary until the time of his departure for Ohio to take employment there. He was always ready to give both time and money, the last minute and penny of his ability to the cause of Socialism. Virginia Socialists and especially the members of Local Strasburg and the State office will feel keenly the loss of Comrade Jenkins. We feel sure that every one of the over six hundred Socialists in the State of Virginia will unite with the Union Star in extending their heartfelt sympathy and condolences to the widow and family.

October 13, 1916

R. A. Tyree, a prominent member of the Socialist Party of Richmond, Va. and member of the State Executive Committee of that party, died at his home there recently. Though but an ordinary workingman, with a workingman's opportunities, he had given a great deal of study to social and economic problems, and never hesitated to express his opinions under any circumstances.

As the death angel was flying thru our community it claimed the little brown eyed Jane, the 2 year and 3 months old daughter of Mr. and Mrs. T. H. Brown. She was taken ill 2 days before she died with infantile paralysis. She died Saturday Sept. 9th at two o'clock p.m., and was laid to rest at her grandfather's at Winfall at 4 o'clock on Saturday with many beautiful flowers, which covered the mound. She leaves father, mother, two brothers and one sister to mourn her loss.

Edge Notes-The death angel visited the home of Mr. and Mrs. Daniel Minix at one o'clock Tuesday the 19th and claimed the little bright blue eyed Mary, who was the picture of health. She was only 2 years, 3 months and 19 days old. She was taken with the dreadful disease, infantile paralysis. The funeral service was conducted by Rev. Mr. Soyars, assisted by Rev. Mr. Barber, of Halifax. She was laid to rest on the little knoll just beyond the home which is the only little mound but which was covered with many beautiful flowers. She leaves father, mother, Aunt Dollie Gilbert, 8 brothers and sisters to mourn her loss.

October 27, 1916

Resolutions of Respect-Mrs. Victoria H. Lawson, Bi-county Superintendent of Press Work of W.C.T.U. of Campbell and Appomattox, died in May 1916. At a recent convention held at Concord the following resolutions were passed:
Whereas, it has pleased our Heavenly Father, in his all-wise providence, to remove from our midst by death our beloved member; therefore be it resolved,
1st, That in the death of sister we have lost a valued and earnest worker, one who was untiring in her devotions to the cause of Temperance.
2nd, That while we shall miss her leadership and her example, that we bow in humble submission to Him who is too wise to err.
3rd, That a copy of there resolutions be spread upon our minutes, a copy sent to the Virginia Call and Union Star and a copy sent to the family.
Mrs. W. A. Rorer,
Miss Lucy Rice,

Miss Catherine Peterson.

November 3, 1916

Abell, Charlotte county, Oct.23.-The death angel entered the home of Mr. and Mrs. Jesse C. Johnston and took from them their darling brown-eyed baby boy, Henry Lee, aged 11 months and 9 days. His death was caused by cholera infantum. It was an unexpected death and a great shock to the family, as he had only been sick two days. He was laid to rest in the Mt. Carmel cemetery Oct.24 at three o'clock p.m., the funeral service being conducted by Rev. G. A. Chocklett.
Besides his mother and father he leaves two sisters and two brothers and other close relatives to mourn his death. All that loving hands could do was done but of no avail.
Dearest Lee thou hast left us,
Now thy loss we deeply feel:
But 'tis God who hath bereft us,
He can all our sorrows heal.
A Friend.

November 10, 1916

On last Thursday morning at six o'clock, Zora Bailey, wife of R. L. Burton, died at her home near Brookneal.
She was a patient sufferer, submissive through her sickness to the Father's will, and when the summons came passed calmly and peacefully away, surrounded by a number of her loved ones.
She was a kind, loving and loyal one, ever ready and willing to help all. One in whom all who knew her had utmost confidence. The respect in which the deceased was held was attested by the large concourse of friends and relatives which gathered to show their last respect to the memory of a friend. She leaves a husband and six children, all boys, father, mother, seven sisters and three brothers.
The funeral service was held in Brookneal Baptist church, conducted by her pastor, Rev. John Bass. The floral contributions were numerous and beautiful.

December 1, 1916

Mrs. Arsella Virginia Driscoll aged 73 years, died Wednesday
morning at her home in Lynchburg. Her body was brought back to
Brookneal yesterday and interred at her old home near here. She
was a sister of G. W. Holt, of this county.

December 8, 1916

Malcolm Edward, the little three year old son of Mr. and Mrs. J. L.
Holt, died at his home near Morris Church last Friday with
diphtheria.

December 15, 1916

Many friends in this and adjoining counties will be pained to learn
of the death of Mrs. John Bustard, which occurred at her home in
Danville last week. Mrs. Bustard was formerly Miss Vina Clarke,
daughter of the late Eppa Clarke, of Halifax county.

December 22, 1916

Mrs. Mary A. Puckett died last Monday morning at 12:30 o'clock
at the home of her daughter, Mrs. J. O. Terry, after a long illness
of many months, at the advanced age of 83 years. She had been a
member of Ebenezer Baptist church nearly all her life, and was a
fervent and earnest Christian. She delighted in the promises of
God, and strove to be resigned to God's will and to be true and
loyal to her Saviour to the last. Her husband was killed in battle
the second year of the civil war. After the death of her husband she
was cared for by her brother, J. R. Holt, and by the aid of the
Masonic order, raised two children. She always maintained a very
high esteem for the Masonic order and requested that only Masons
should act as pall bearers at her funeral. Upon the marriage of her
youngest daughter to J. O. Terry, she made her home with them
and helped to raise a large family of grandchildren who in turn
arise to call her blessed and will ever cherish and love her
memory, having bestowed on her to the last every care and
devotion. Her funeral was conducted at the Baptist church
Tuesday, Dec. 19th by the writer, and she was laid to rest in the

Wickliffe cemetery.
W. S. Royall.

Death of Prominent Socialist-Death of J. P. Taylor, of Winston-Salem, a Loss to Movement
The Union Star has just been informed of the death of J. P. Taylor, of Winston-Salem, N.C. The Winston-Salem Journal, of Dec. 10, gave quite a lengthy account of the funeral of Mr. Taylor, from which we take the following paragraphs:
"Mr. Taylor was born in Henrico county, Va., September 21, 1856, the son of the late H. P. and Mrs. Cornelia Taylor. Following the completion of his education in Richmond, he came to this city in 1884 and accepted a position with the tobacco firm of Taylor, Ledbetter & Company, of which his brother, Mr. W. B. Taylor, was a member. After the dissolution of this firm, Messrs. W. B. and J. P. Taylor formed the firm of Taylor Brothers, tobacco manufacturers, which is one of the most successful and substantial businesses of the city.
"Mr. Taylor was one of the most highly respected and dearly loved Christian men in Winston-Salem, his endeavors having always been to advance the interests and help the conditions of the working people. He has been a faithful and consistent member of the First Presbyterian church in this city since moving here and had always contributed liberally of his splendid means to his church and to others in the city, as well as to all charitable and benevolent causes.
"One of the most distinguishing marks of this noble and admirable man was his prominence and enthusiasm as a Socialist, not of the extreme or abnormally radical type, but a conscientious and workable Socialism, which he thought would benefit the laboring man. It was this spirit that prompted him and his brother to increase the wages in their factory and shorten the hours of the workers. "Mr. Taylor is survived by a wife and five children; two daughters; Misses Jane Marshall and Pauline Wharton Taylor; three sons: Messrs. Charles, Edward, and J. P. Taylor, Jr.; two sisters: Mrs. Sidney Adair and Miss Cornelia Taylor of Richmond; two brothers Mr. W. B. Taylor of Richmond.

January 5, 1917

Mrs. L. H. Joy, who was Miss Lillie E. Sublett before her marriage, died at 4 o'clock a.m. Jan.1st, at St. Luke's hospital Richmond, Va., where she had been under treatment for some time. The deceased was 35 years old and was loved by every one that knew her.

Mrs. Joy is survived by her husband and little daughter, Sarah, and the following brothers and sisters: W. T. Sublett, of Morris Church; N. S. Sublett, of Brookneal; C. B. Sublett, of Roanoke; Mrs. M. E. Gyllenflyck and Miss Flossie Sublett, of Lynchburg, and Mrs. B. W. Johnson of Stone Mountain, The funeral took place at Union Hill Baptist church, of which she was a member, conducted by her pastor, Rev. Mr. Brook.

January 12, 1917

Edge, Jan.7.- Mrs. E. H. Cothran died at her home Friday afternoon at 2 o'clock after an illness of about ten months. She was laid to rest at Edge Hill Baptist church by the side of her four children. She leaves her husband, one daughter, Bertha, and five sons, John, Sam, Frank, Joe, and Jesse, and several sisters.

Naruna, Va., Jan.8.- A telegram was received here last week announcing the death of Guss Evans, who died on Wednesday in New Mexico, where he had been for more than twelve months for his health. His wife had been by his bedside for about three months.

He was born in Appomattox county. After he was married to Miss Annie Gilliam, he made his home in Newport News for a few years. After leaving there, he made his home in Ensley, Ala., until his death.

He leaves six daughters: Mrs. Ivor Walsh, Mrs. Ercell Moran, Misses Thelma, Grace, Ruth, and Dorothy Evans, his wife, father and mother, Mr. and Mrs. John Evans; sisters, Mrs. W.S. Brown and Mrs. Walker Coleman; and five brothers, Jesse, John, Jr., Luther, Carrington and Tom to mourn their loss. Interment was made at Ensley, Ala.

February 2, 1917

Dr. W.O. Tune spent last week in the home of his mother, Mrs.
Jennie Tune. He was called there by the illness and death of his
aunt, Miss Pattie Tune.

Emette Carwile, of Naruna, aged 57 years, died last Saturday night
at 8 o'clock at St. Andrews Hospital in Lynchburg where he was
taken last August for treatment. He underwent an operation the 9th
of August and again in October, but he steadily grew worse until
the end came.
Mr. Carwile is survived by his wife and seven children and other
relatives. He united with Sharon Methodist church early in life. At
the time of his death he was a member of Mt. Zion Methodist
church on the Campbell circuit. He suffered intensely from the
time he was first taken sick, but he bore his affliction patiently and
said he was ready to go.
His body was brought to the home of his brother, Lee Carwile, of
Naruna, on Sunday and on Monday the funeral services were
conducted at 2 o'clock at Sharon church by the pastor Rev. W. C.
Harris after which interment was made in the Sharon cemetery.

Death of Baby Boy-The little ten-month old baby of Mr. and Mrs.
Eulee Jennings died Sunday, Jan. 28th, after a short illness. He
was laid to rest at Ebenezer cemetery, Rev. P. O. Soyars
conducting the service. The sorrowing parents have the sympathy
of their friends and the entire neighborhood.

February 16, 1917

Samuel A. Lawson, the well known merchant of Hat Creek, near
Brookneal, died Tuesday night at his home. He had been ill but a
short time, but his condition was not considered serious and death
came as a shock to his family and friends. Mr. Lawson was 47
years old. He is survived by his wife who was Miss Mollie
Hobson, and nine living children.
The burial took place Thursday afternoon and notwithstanding the
bad weather, was attended by a large concourse of friends. A
delegation of Elks from Lynchburg, and of Odd Fellows from
Brookneal attended the funeral, the deceased being a member of

these orders.

On Feb.9th the death angel entered the home of David R. Marshall claiming him as its victim. He had been ill for a long time while with a disease that baffled the skill of many physicians that had attended him, they being unable to locate his disease. Everything that loving hearts and willing hands could do was done, but they could not stay the hand of death, and he bore his sufferings without a murmur. He was the son of the late Carles and Mary Marshall and was in the 45th year of his age, having been born Oct. 10, 1872. On Nov.7, 1912, he was married to Miss Nannie Dodd, who survives him with a little daughter, Bessie. The following sisters also survive him: Mmes. E. H. Holt, J. W. Wood and O. W. Holt. He was a consistent member of the Presbyterian church at Hat Creek. His remains were interred in the cemetery at Falling church Saturday afternoon, the funeral service being conducted by his pastor, Rev. J. A. Scott. The pall bearers were Henry Lee Foster, Collins Clark, Sandy Foster, J. A. Ingram, Nowlin Elder, Charles and E. W. McDowell and Charlie Midkiff.

February 23, 1917

Mrs. W. M. Barnes, of Christiansburg, who attended the funeral of her cousin, S. A. Lawson, returned Monday to her home.

Resolutions of Respect-In the memory of Brother S. A. Lawson, who died February 14, 1917.
Once again, death hath summoned a Brother Odd Fellow, and the golden gateway to the Eternal City has opened to welcome him to his home. He has completed his work in the ministering to the wants of the afflicted, in shedding light into darkened souls and in bringing joy into places of misery, and as his reward has received the plandit "welldone," from the Supreme Master.
And whereas, the all-wise and merciful Master of the universe has called our beloved and respected brother home, and he having been a true and faithful member of our beloved Order, therefore be it
Resolved, That Brookneal Lodge, No. 267, I.O.O.F., of Brookneal, Virginia, in testimony of her loss, be draped in mourning for thirty days and that we tender to the family of our deceased brother our

sincere condolence in their deep affliction, and that a copy of these resolutions be sent to the family, a copy spread on the minutes of the Lodge and a copy published in the Union Star.

W. H. Ginther,
W. W. Rudder,
S. T. Holt,
Committee

March 9, 1917

Mrs. T. L. Foster died at her home near Brookneal last Saturday and was buried Sunday afternoon in the Foster burying ground. Mrs. Foster, who was Miss Dollie A. Woolridge, of Appomattox county, before her marriage, is survived by her husband and seven children. She had been in bad health for sometime but her death came rather suddenly and was quite a shock to the family. Mrs. Foster had been a consist and devoted member of Union Hill Baptist church for nearly twenty years.

Aged Negress Badly Burned-Mary Williams, colored, about 70 years of age, was probably fatally burned Tuesday when her clothing caught fire from the grate in the home of Mrs. R. E. Gilliam where she was employed as cook. Had it not been for the present of mind of Mrs. Gilliam who was in the room at the time and snatched the blankets from the bed and threw them over the old woman she would probably have been burned to death. After extinguishing the flames, Mrs. Gilliam phoned for a doctor but it happened that both Drs. Williams and Tune were out of town, so Harold Thornton, of Thornton's Pharmacy rendered first aid and made the sufferer as comfortable as possible until Dr. Tune could reach her. While everything possible is being done for her little hope is held out for her recovery. Aunt Mary was a slave in the family of Wirt Williams' parents and she remained with the Williams family until a few years ago when she came to Brookneal and for the past four years had made her home with Mrs. Gilliam.

Card of Thanks-We desire to extend our sympathy and heartfelt thanks to many good friends who were so faithful and attentive during the illness, death and burial of our beloved wife and mother.

T. L. Foster and Family

March 16, 1917

A Card of Thanks-We desire to express our sincere thanks for the many acts of kindness shown us during the illness and death of our son, Leonard.

Mr. & Mrs. Henry Guthrie, Clarkton, Va.

March 30, 1917

The saddest day which ever entered the home of Mr. and Mrs. Henry Guthrie was the evening of March 6th, when the death angel took away their son, Leonard, aged 12 years. The little fellow was only sick about 3 weeks. All was done for him that loving hands and hearts could do, and his mother stood by his bed night after night and day after day waiting anxiously for his recovery. But God knew best and we feel that it is for some good purpose he was taken away. He was always bright and cheerful at home and at school. He leaves to mourn his loss his father, mother, three sisters, and four brothers. On Wednesday following his death at 3 o'clock p.m., his remains were laid to rest in the Guthrie burying ground near Perth. The family have the sympathy of their many friends in their sad bereavement.

Mary Tribble, Clarkton, Va.

Death of Aged Colored Woman-Aunt Mary Williams, the aged colored woman who was so badly burned three weeks ago at the home of R. E. Gilliam when her clothing caught on fire from the grate, died Sunday afternoon at 3 o'clock, the end coming peacefully after much suffering. She was buried at Green Spring Monday afternoon.

April 6, 1917

Houston, Va., March 31(Special)-W. O. Lovelace, a prominent citizen of this county, who resided near this place, died last night. He was seventy-two years of age and had lived in this county all of his life. He was a past master of Vernon Hill lodge of Mason's, had been a member of the Virginia Legislature, magistrate and commissioner of the revenue, and also served as a Confederate soldir (soldier) in the Civil War. Mr. Lovelace leaves a widow and a lage (large) number of relatives besides a host of friends. He was widely known and well liked by all for his many commendable traits of character.

April 13, 1917

Death of Aged Colored Man-Watt Spraggins, a well known and respected negro of the old regime, died at his home in Halifax county last Monday after an illness of two days.

April 20, 1917

A gloom of profound sorrow was cast over our town Tuesday when the news was received that Mr. William Anderson Rice of this place had died Monday night at 8:30 o'clock at the home of Mr. and Mrs. S. D. Unstead, in Lynchburg.
Mr. Rice was 36 years of age and had been a resident of Brookneal for a number of years. He had been employed by the American Tobacco Company to teach the natives of Rhodesia, South Africa to grow tobacco. He spent several years there, during which he contracted a fever from the effects of which he never recovered. He was in Lynchburg for treatment at the time of his death. The remains were brought to Brookneal Tuesday, and from here they were taken to Bethel church, Charlotte county, for interment, Wednesday. W. D. Diuguid, funeral director of Lynchburg, was in charge. The floral offerings were many and beautiful.
The pall bearers were: J. H. Foster, N. I. Walthall, A. T. Thornton, Frank Williams, E. T. Yeaman and Owen Armstead. The flower bearers were: Mrs. Jere White, Mrs. N. I. Walthall, Miss Effie Webb, Mrs. J. E. Webb, Mrs. R. F. Connalley, Miss Thalia White and Miss Bessie Berkley. The services wore conducted jointly by Revs. John B. Williams, G. A. Chocklett and F. M. Ryburn.
The deceased is survived by his wife, who was Miss Ethel Lawson, and one son, W. A. Rice, Jr., his father, W. D. Rice, of Charlotte county, one brother, A. H. Rice, also of Charlotte county, one sister, Mrs. Horace Anderson, of Crewe, and eight half-sisters and brothers.

April, 27, 1917

Thomas Cardwell, a highly respected colored man, aged 72 years, died at his home near here after a short illness.

May 11, 1917

Mrs. Martha A. Elder, widow of Lewallen Elder, died at her home three miles from this place, on May 2.
The burial services were conducted by Rev. P. O. Soyars, of Gladys on May 4th, in the Ebeneezer cemetery.
Mrs. Elder, before her marriage was Miss Martha Foster. She was 84 years old and is survived by seventy-four grandchildren, eleven great grandchildren and twelve children. Her surviving children are: J. W. Elder, Mrs. Emma Mason and S. B. Elder, of Brookneal; Mrs. B. E. P. Poole, R. L. Elder and Mrs. C. W. Hunter of Naruna; Mrs. J. B. Suddith, George W. Elder, Chas. O. Elder, Sylvester Elder, Wm. H. Elder and Mrs. Roxanna Monroe, of Gladys.

May 18, 1917

Many friends in this community will be pained to learn of the death of James R. Gilliam, a prominent business man of Lynchburg, which occurred at his home in that city Wednesday afternoon. Mr. Gilliam was a native of Campbell county, but spent his young manhood in Amherst county where his mother moved soon after his father's death.

Death of Little Child-The little three year old child of C. S. Daniel which had been suffering from pellagra for several weeks, died yesterday morning and will be buried today.

In Memoriam-Henderson-In sad but loving remembrance of Edgar H. Henderson, who departed this life one year ago, May 13, 1916.
The twinkling stars are beaming
Upon a silent grave
Where sleeps without dreaming
The one I could not save
O! memory of that evening

As we stood with aching hearts
Knowing the one I loved so dearly
Was pierced by death's cold dart.
Just one year ago you left us,
Still I miss your smiling face,
And often in hours of solitude
Starts the unbidden tears.
By his Loving Wife

May 25, 1917

Mrs. Jack Pillow, of Wren, died Thursday morning after a
prolonged illness. She is survived by her husband and a large
family.

June 1, 1917

Miss Rosa Waugh, of Lynchburg, came down as a friend of the
family to attend the burial of W. B. Scott.

Our community was pained and shocked early Monday morning to
learn that W. B. Scott, of Seven Islands, had died the previous
night after an illness of about an hour from heart trouble.
William Bailey Scott was the third son of the late Patrick H. Scott
and was in the 60th year of his age at the time of his death. He was
born and reared and always lived on Seven Islands farm in the
border of Halifax county near Brookneal. For the past twelve years
he has made his home with his brother, the late F. A. Scott. He had
not enjoyed robust health for several months but was able to attend
to his affairs and was present at the services in the Presbyterian
church Sunday afternoon.
He was possessed of a cheerful disposition and was always ready
with a merry jest and witty repartee in greetings with his friends,
most of whom affectionately called him "Uncle Bill." He is
survived by two brothers and two sisters, C. C. Scott, of
Brookneal; C. Y. Scott and Mrs. R. R. Todd, of Seven Islands, and
Mrs. S. B. Yuille, of Norfolk.
The funeral service was conducted at the home of Rev. G. W.
Ribble on Tuesday afternoon and the interment was in the Scott
burying lot. A large number of sympathizing friends attended the

obsequies as a mark of respect to his memory, many and beautiful were the floral tributes. The pall bearers were: E. T. Yeaman, W. R. Walker, R. F. Connally, C. S. Stephens, W. O. Tune and W. C. Walker. The flower bearers were E. R. Monroe, Jere White, B. J. Bomar, W. G. Puckett, W. E. Elmore and C. W. Harvey.

June 8, 1917

Mrs. C. C. Adams died at Staunton Wednesday. She was about 60 years of age and was Miss Mittie Francis before her marriage. She is survived by her husband and two daughters, Mrs. O. R. Graves, of Huddleston, and Miss Lena Adams, of Danville; and four brothers, R. F. Francis, of Brookneal; John Francis, of Long Island; Willie Francis, of Nathalie; and W. S. Francis, of Gladys.

Seneca Notes-The four months old baby boy of Mrs. Hunt, who was visiting home-folk here died last week.

June 15, 1917

A report has been received here announcing the death of Mrs. Dora Read, of Gladys.

July 6, 1917

Miss Kate Younger died on last Wednesday and was buried in the family burying ground near her home. She was a member of McKendree Methodist church. She lived a long and useful life.

July 13, 1917

A special grand jury brought in an indictment against Thomas F. Scruggs, former chief of police of Altavista, charging him with the murder of his wife, Hattie Taylor Scruggs, on the night of June 9th. Mrs. Scruggs was shot and killed at her home in Altavista, while in bed with her husband, who claimed that she shot herself. The trial of Scruggs will begin today.

Mrs. Jim Thomas and daughter, Selma, were called to Greenville, N.C., last Thursday by the death of her little granddaughter.

Mrs. W. Clowdis' two year old baby died last week. We extend our deepest sympathy to the family in their sorrow.

The infant son of Mr. Ernest Blanks, of Republican Grove, died Saturday and was buried in the family burying ground Sunday. Rev. W.T. Creath conducted the funeral services.

Mr. John Covington, one of the community's oldest citizens, died at his home near Rosa Sunday night and will be buried Tuesday afternoon in the family burying ground near his old home. He was a member of McKendree Methodist church.

July 20, 1917

The little child of Mr. and Mrs. C. W. Coates, died and was buried last Sunday.

July 27, 1917

"Aunt" Lucy Hamlet, an esteemed colored woman, who lived to a ripe old age at Hat Creek, died Sunday morning and was buried Monday afternoon at New Hat Creek cemetery.

A horrible murder was committed near Red House last Monday, Albert Barrett, colored, and his fourteen-year-old son slaying Mr. W. T. Roach, white, a young farmer. Considerable excitement was caused. Several hundred men of both Charlotte and Campbell counties prrticipated (participated) in catching the murderers. They were caught Thursday near Rustburg. Their trail will be at Charlotte Court House on Thursday, the 26th inst.

Both to Die in the Chair-At a special term of the circuit court held at Charlotte C.H. yesterday, Judge Hundley presiding, Albert Barrett, colored, was sentenced to die in the electric chair on August 31st, for the murder of W. T. Roach, near Red House, Va., a few days ago. Barrett's seventeen year old son was also sentenced to die in the chair on the same day for his part in the crime. The trial started at 10 o'clock a.m., and lasted until 3 p.m. Ten witnesses were examined. The jury was out only fifteen minutes.

Soldier Killed While on Duty-Robert E. Crane, a member of Troop C 1st Virginia Cavalry, was killed while doing guard duty at the Scott's Creek Bridge on the Virginian Railway, near Cullen, sometime between 9:30 Saturday night and 1 o'clock Sunday morning. He had gone on detail duty at 9:30, and when the relief arrived at 1 a.m., Crane was nowhere to be found. He made no answer to repeated calls and after considerable search had been made no evidence of his whereabouts of what happened to him was found except his hat. At day break Sunday morning his dead body was found by the track. There was a fracture on the left side of his head and the back of his head was quite badly bruised. There was also a cut on his chin. Beyond this, other than a few minor scratches, the body was not mangled. It is thought, however, that he was killed by a passing train.

The body of the dead soldier was taken to Richmond Sunday afternoon, accompanied by a detail which remained for the funeral. A detail from the soldiers stationed in Richmond met the body at the train. Mr. Crane had been a member of this troop since April and was a young man of exemplary habits and a fine soldier.

Miss Annie Chaney, the fifteen-year-old daughter of Mr. Josh Chaney, died Friday morning after an illness of six weeks. She was a member of Millstone church and was very attentive in Sunday school. She leaves a mother, father, several sisters and brothers besides many friends to mourn her loss. She was buried in the family burying ground near Republican Grove. Rev. Mr. Royall, of Danville, conducted the burial services.

August 4, 1917

Mr. Arthur Dickerson died Sunday morning after an illness of several months. Mr. Dickerson was taken to Richmond for an operation last week. He leaves a mother, father, several sisters and brothers and a wife and two children to mourn their loss. Mr. Dickerson was a member of McKendree Methodist church, where he was buried Monday afternoon. He had been in ill health for several years.

35

A colored man named Will Rosser died last Friday, of heart trouble.

August 10, 1917

Hat Creek Happenings -Little Royal, the infant son of Mr. and Mrs. Walter Blanks, did (died) Saturday night at 1:20 o'clock, aged 13 months.

We were sorry to hear of the death of Mr. Dwight Gilliland on the 28th of July.

Death of an Infant-Royal Herbert, the infant son of Mr. and Mrs. Walter E. Blanks, died at their home near Hat Creek early Sunday morning. He was thirteen months old and although quite young had won for himself a host of friends who were grieved at his sudden passing away. The funeral services were conducted by Rev. Fisher, of Lynchburg. "Someday we'll understand," "Over there," and "Safe in the arms of Jesus" were sung at the church. Messrs. Henry Lee Foster, Thomas Elder, Anthony Carey and Robert Reynolds acted as pall bearers. The body was laid away in the burying grounds of Beulah church, late Sunday afternoon. Mr. and Mrs. Blanks and their little ones have our sympathy in their sad bereavement. We know their baby is gone but not forgotten, but little Royal has gone
To a land where sorrows cease,
Where there there is happiness and peace;
Where there is joy and endless rest
Forever among the blest.
There is a home all bright and fair,
And Christ and his redeemed are there:
No darkness comes, no pain nor sin;
And he hath entered in.
There rapturous praises fill the air,
Celestial ones, all bright and fair,
Forever sing around the throne
Where he hath gone.
And there with loved ones gone before
We meet again to part no more;
There Jesus calls the loved ones home,

Aud bade him come.
Then, shall we call him back again.

August 24, 1917

Mr. L. W. Dunivant was stricken with paralysis on last Thursday
and died Friday evening. He was buried on Saturday morning,
Rev. A. Rolen officiating. Mr. Dunivant was 74 years old, he was
a member of Franklin M.E. church, an old confederate veteran,
and universally respected and esteemed by his neighbors. His wife
preceded him to the grave by a good many years.

August 31,1917

The community was shocked last Sunday morning when the death
angel entered the home of Mr. and Mrs. Johnnie Crews and took
from them their nineteen-year-old daughter, Mamie. She was only
sick a few days. She is survived by her father and mother, three
sisters and three brothers and leaves a host of friends to mourn
their loss. The remains were laid to rest in the family burying
ground, where a large crowd witnessed the last rites. She was a
popular young lady and will be greatly missed in this community.
She was loved by all who knew her. We extend our heartfelt
sympathy to the bereaved family.

Wren Writings-Mr. Tom Mann, who died at his home, near
Brookneal, was laid to rest in Midway burying ground on last
Friday afternoon. The funeral services were conducted by Rev. Dr.
Scott, of Lynchburg. "Asleep in Jesus" and "Gather at the River"
were sung at the grave. The pall bearers were Willie St. John,
Paulette Smith, Otis Morrison, Burrel Henderson, Bob Davidson
and Homer Coleman. Mr. Mann is survived by his wife, three
sons, six daughters, one brother and two sisters. The sorrowing
ones have the sympathy of the entire neighbor in their
bereavement.

The death angel visited the home of Mr. and Mrs. J. W. Crews
Sunday and claimed for its own their nineteen year old daughter,
Mamie. Her death was a shock to the community, as she was only
ill for a few days.

Card of Thanks-Mrs. Thomas Mann and family wish to thank the many kind friends and neighbors who were so nice and kind to them during the illness, death and burial of their husband and father, William Thomas Mann, who departed this life Aug.22, 1917.

September 7, 1917

We were very sorry to hear of the death of Mr. Jamie Hill, which was very much of a surprise to all.

September 14, 1917

Mr. Glover Martin died of typhoid fever last Friday and was buried at Gladys on Saturday afternoon in Kedron church cemetery.

September 28, 1917

The death angel visited in the home of Mr. Wesley Elder and took from him his beloved wife.

We are sorry to learn of Mr. Jim McIvor's death.

October 5, 1917

Joe Mason, of near Sugar Hill, died last night about 8 o'clock, after a lingering illness. Interment will be made at Falling church this afternoon. Mr. Mason is survived by his wife and one son, Franklin, and five daughters, Misses Vetie, Minnie and Dollie, and Mrs. L. W. Guthrie and Mrs. W. C. Donald.

The infant daughter of Mr. and Mrs. Eva Saunders, of this place, died Sept.28th and burried (buried) at the Baptist cemetery, Staurday (Saturday) Sept. 29th.

Mrs. R. D. Burks, who has been sick for some time, died at her home Friday morning, her remains were carried to Lynchburg for burial.

Mrs. Mary Rickman, widow of J. Hubbard Rickman, died Sept. 25th. She leaves one daughter, Mrs. John Throckmorton. She was burried (buried) at Crystal Hill Baptist church cemetery Sept. 26th. Funeral services conducted by Mr. Ambrose.

October 12, 1917

Mr. T. E. Dickerson, of South Boston, died last Tuesday after an illness of two days. Mr. Dickerson had been in bad health for some time and on last Monday he had a stroke of paralysis from which he never recovered. He was brought to McKendree Methodist church, of which he had been an active member for a long time, for burial. He was buried by the Masons. He is survived by his widow, one son and four daughters.

News was received here of the death of Taw Hurt, brother-in-law of Mrs. R. O. Elder, in Lynchburg Sunday.

Mr. Tommie Guthrie, who has been afflicted for the past twenty years, died not long since. We all deeply sympathize with his family in their trouble.

Mr. Tom Dickinson, of South Boston, died Wednesday of last week, and was buried on Friday at McKendree church under the auspices of the Masonic order.

October 19, 1917

Dropped Dead-A report reached Brookneal yesterday that Mr. Alex Seymore, who lived near Nathalie, dropped dead on the fair grounds at South Boston Wednesday. Heart failure is supposed to have been the cause. Mr. Seymore was about 78 years of age.

News has been received here of the death of Mrs. John Elam, in Texas. Mrs. Elam was formerly Lizzie Nowlin, and was first married to a Mr. Stratton. After his death she married Mr. Elam. She resided near Brookneal on the Campbell and Charlotte county line until sbout (about) a year ago when she went to Texas to reside with relatives.

Mr. and Mrs. W. W. Averette Jr., were called to Farville last
Friday by the death of Mrs. Averette's brother, David B. Ligon.

November 2, 1917

Mrs. Tom Bray, of Richmond, died last Monday. The body was
brought to Millstone Baptist church for burial. She had been a
member there for several years and attended Sunday school
regularly until she moved to Richmond. Mr. Logan Ray, of
Meadville, conducted the funeral services. Mrs. Bray died on her
17th birthday. She was married in February and since that time,
she has made her home in Richmond, where Mr. Bray is engaged
in business. She leaves a husband, mother and father, several
sisters and brothers and many friends to mourn their loss.

Our hearts were greatly saddened when on the 7th of September,
the Death Angel came and took from us our own dear one, Grover
H. Martin, aged 25 years. He is survived by his wife and three
little children, Raymond, Lena and Annie, also his father, three
brothers and two sisters. His brothers are John, Gilbert and Robert,
all of Gladys, and his sisters are Mrs. Roy Dudley and Mrs. Bill
Roakes, both of Gladys. All that willing hands could do to keep
with us this dear husband and father was done, but God knows
best. He had been ill with typhoid fever for seven weeks and
gradually grew weaker until the end. Interment was made in
Kedron cemetery of which church he was a member. "Happy
Day" and "Safe in the Arms of Jesus," were sung in the church,
and "Shall we Gather at the river" and "O, think of the home over
there," were sung at the grave. We miss this dear one but we know
that he has only fallen asleep in Jesus. Why should we weep when
this dear one sleeps on the bosom of the Savior in the mansions of
glory prepared for the blessed, for death is only a dream.
Sleep on beloved, sleep and take thy rest,
Lay down thy head upon the Saviors breast:
We loved thee well, but Jesus loved thee best
Good night! Good night!

We are sorry to learn of the death of Mr. Wheeler Pugh.

November 16, 1917

Mrs. Joe Terry, of near Mullbery, died the 6 of Nov., and was burried (buried) at Mullbery Cemetery on the 7th. She leaves a husband, four boys and one girl to mourn her death. She was a member of the Baptist church and will be missed by her many friends.

We were very sorry to learn of the death of Mrs. Nate Cox, who before her last marriage was Mrs. Jordan, mother of W. T. Jordan. She was burried (buried) at Whites Chappel (Chapel) Friday afternoon.

Thomas F. Scruggs, former chief of police of Altavista, who was tried here last week for the murder of his wife, was given ten years in the penitentiary.

The home of Mr. Joe LaPrade was made sad on Sunday night when the death angel entered and claimed their aged father, Mr. John C. LaPrade. Mr. LaPrade had been in bad health for a good many years, but his death was a shock to his many friends. He was in his 83rd year. He was a member of the M.E. church and will be missed by his many friends. He leaves five sons and three daughters to mourn his death.
Dearest father, thou has left us
And our loss we deeply feel,
But 'tis God that has bereft us,
He can all our sorrows heal.
Yet again we hope to meet thee
When the day of life is fled,
When in Heaven in joy to greet thee
Where no farewell tear is shed.
"A Friend"

Mrs. Martha Cocke died at her home on Wednesday, Nov. 7th. She had been confined to her bed for about two months, but had been an invalid for two years or more. She leaves five daughters and one son to mourn her death, Miss Dora Cocke, of Roanoke Rapid, Misses Rosa and Annie Cocke of Wren Jean, West., Va., Miss Janie Cocke of Victoria; Mrs. N. T. Cocke and Mr. Walter

Jordan, of Phenix.
A precious one from as has gone
The voice we love is still.
A place is vacant in our home
Which never can be filled.

November 23, 1917

Rustburg. Nov.19.- The circuit court here during Friday and
Saturday was engaged in the trial of the suit to contest the will of
Chas. Chas. H. Foster, of the Hat Creek neighborhood, who left an
estate of some $5,000.00, which by the will he gave to Mrs. Eula
L. Foster, the wife of C. A. Foster. Mrs. Eula L. Foster was the
niece of Chas. H. Foster. The decedent had no children and had
taken Mrs. Eula L. Foster when she was a child and her parents
died and reared her.
The will was contested by Anthony Foster and others, a brother
and the nieces and nephews of Mr. Foster. R. H. Willis of
Roanoke appeared for the contestants of the will and A. H. Light
appeared for Mrs. Eula L. Foster.
After being argued the case was submitted to the jury about 4
o'clock in the afternoon. It was a special jury selected for the
purpose of trying the case and their verdict was in favor of the
validity of the will.

November 30, 1917

Card of Thanks-Mr. C. E. Tucker wishes to express his sincere
thanks and appreciation to the good people of Brookneal and
vicinity, and especially to the ladies of the Eastern Star and the
W.C.T.U. for their kindness and sympathetic consideration during
the illness, death and burial of his wife, Mrs. Hallie Marshall
Tucker.

Death of an Aged Colored Woman-Aunt Sallie Walker, probably
one of the oldest colored women in this section of the country died
at the home of her son in Brookneal Thursday morning at an early
hour. Her age was unknown but old people of Brookneal say she
was an old woman when they were children, so she must have
been near the century mark.

Mr. John Marshall died the night of the 23rd and was burried (buried) at Mullberry Cemetery on Saturday.

An old colored man, John Jennings, of this place, died on Monday night. He was about 84 years of age.

Mrs. Jim Edmunds, of near Cody, died the 20th and was buried on the 21st at Mr. Jim Edmunds, Sr.'s home. She leaves a husband and four small children and a mother and one sister. She had been sick for several weeks. She was 28 years old.

Mrs. Phil Guthrie and daughters, Daisy and Lenis, and Mr. W. F. Jordan were called to Lynchburg last Wednesday to attend the burial of their niece, Fowler Jordan. She had only been sick a few days and her death came as a surprise to her many relatives and friends. She was eight years old and leaves her father, besides many friends and relatives to mourn her death.

The death angel entered the home of Mr. Jim Edmunds last Tuesday morning at 8:30 snd (and) took from him his beloved wife. Besides relatives and friends she is survived by her husband and four small children. They have the deepest sympathy of the community.

Miss Myrtle Walthall has planted flowers on her mothers grave, thereby showing her loving remembrance of her departed parent.

December 7, 1917

Mr. John W. Marshall, a highly respected citizen was buried Nov. 24 at Mulberry cemetery. He was a valued member of Mulberry church. He leaves a wife, three brothers and one sister besides a host of friends to mourn his loss.

December 14, 1917

We have heard of the sad death of one of our soldier boys, Marvin Gough. He enlisted in the Navy three weeks ago and died early this week in a Norfolk hospital of typhoid pneumonia. He left a wife and one child who have our deepest sympathy in their great trouble.

December 21, 1917

Mrs. Mary L. Ginther, wife of W. H. Ginther, died at her home here at about 10 o'clock last Thursday night after a brief illness. She was in her 25th year, had only been married about two years and was very much devoted to her husband and home.
Mrs. Ginther was the daughter of Mr. and Mrs. A. Candler, of 1113 Monroe St., Lynchburg. She was a member of the First Baptist Church in that city. The body was taken to Lynchburg Friday where it was embalmed at Duiguid's undertaking parlors. The funeral took place Sunday afternoon at 2:30 at the home of her parents and the services were conducted by Rev. W. W. Hamilton, D. D. After the funeral services the body was laid to rest in the family plot in the Presbyterian cemetery.
Mrs. Ginther is survived by her husband, her parents and four brothers and six sisters.

Mrs. Vashti Wingfield, aged 56, widow of the late Robert Wingfield, died Sunday at her home near Naruna. She was stricken with paralysis about three weeks ago and this resulted in her death. Mrs. Wingfield's husband preceded her to the grave about eighteen years ago. The funeral was conducted Monday afternoon at 3 o'clock, by Rev. A. I. Caudle, of Naruna, assisted by Revs. W. C. Harris and J. B. Williams, of Brookneal. Interment was made in the old home burying ground. Mrs. Wingfield is survived by a son and daughter, Mr. C. W. Wingfield and Miss Olive Wingfield; also two brothers, Messrs. John W. and C. O. Scott. She was an amiable Christian woman and well liked by all who knew her.

Little Fannie Neal died at her home last Monday morning about 6 o'clock. Her death was very sudden. She was buried Tuesday afternoon in the family burying ground of this place.

December 28, 1917

Mrs. Lelia Davis, widow of a former newspaper man, died at her home in Chatham Wednesday, from paralysis. She was a sister of Mrs. M. J. Wickliffe, of Brookneal.

Clayton L. Foster, 18 years of age, son of Mr. L.T. Foster, died in a Lynchburg hospital Tuesday morning from pneumonia, resulting from an operation for tonsilitis. He was well known in Brookneal, where he lived for several years.

January 11, 1918

On the morning of the seventh, death entered the home of Mr. D. N. Brooks and claimed for its victim his wife, Mrs. Fannie Brooks. The deceased will be greatly missed in the church and community, for although feeble in health she was a regular attendant at church and Sunday school.

January 18, 1918

Death of a Respected Colored Woman-"Aunt Lizzie" Reid, wife of Rev. L. R. Reid, colored, died at her home near Rabat in Halifax county last Sunday after a lingering illness of more than a year from a complication of diseases. She was widely known and respected by both white and colored people.

Cedar Forest-Mrs. Bradner, who has been extremely ill for some time, died last Monday night. She was buried Wednesday at her home.

Mr. Charles Rice was made sad by the death of his son, William R. Rice, at Camp Lee, which occurred January 11. He was just in the bloom of his life, being 23 years of age. He will be missed very much by his friends and kindred. His body was brought back to his home where it was laid in its last resting place by his brothers of the W.O.W., of which he was a faithful member. The father and brothers have the heartfelt sympathy of this community.

Childrey- Am very sorry to learn of the sad death of Mrs. D. N.Brooks, of Gladys. She was a good Christian woman and loved by everyone who knew her.

January 25, 1918

Mrs. Fannie Brooks, wife of Mr. D. N. Brooks, died at her home at Gladys, Va. on January 7th, 1918, aged 62 years. She had been in feeble health for a number of years, and though at times the worst was feared by her family her death at the time of its occurrence was rather unexpected.
Mrs. Brooks had long been a member of Kedron Baptist church,

was a faithful attendent upon all of its services, a zealous worker in Sunday school, and to say she was loyal in its every demand upon her is but a feeble expression of her fidelity. In the community too, in which she resided, her light as a Christian shone brightly, as a neighbor she was unsurpassed, for in the sick room the fragrance of her presence was felt, and often, so often, a vase of flowers or a waiter of dainties, the thought and work of her mind and hands, lent cheer and comfort to the heart of the restless sufferer. She was likewise one of the pastor's best friends; the writer can testify to this fact, having been closely associated with her for a period of ten years.

She was a tender, lovable woman and the loss occasioned by her death is a heavy one both to her church and the community as well as to her beloved home.

Mrs. Brooks was formerly a Miss Maddox, of Campbell county, and in her girlhood she was married to Mr. D. N. Brooks, also of Campbell, by whom she is survived. She realized that the end was near and expressed her readiness to depart, as indeed she had been heard to do in other days, knowing that "the earthly house of this tabernacle must be dissolved."

On the afternoon of January 8th her funeral service was held at Kedron Baptist church conducted by her pastor, Rev. P. O. Sayars, assisted by Rev. J. A. Barnhardt, of Keysville, former pastor of the deceased; after the funeral, in the presence of a large number of friends and acquaintances, her remains were interred in the cemetery near by, where repose the ashes of other loved ones. It was with sad experience of earth and joyous anticipation of Heaven that we turned away from this flower-covered mound and sought the dreary, desolate home formerly cheered and beautified by her presence.

As we write our hearts go out in sympathy to the stricken husband with whom she had walked, hand in hand, along life's pathway for almost fifty years; also to her five children to whom she was a most tender, devoted mother, whose names are as follows: Mrs. Fitz Moore, of Lynchburg; Mrs. Mack Guy, of Danville: Mr Davis Brooks, of West Virginia: Mr. John Brooks and Mrs. Eugene Organ of Gladys. She also leaves two brothers and one sister, namely, Mr. Joe Maddox, of Lynchburg; and Mr.-Maddox, of Hopewell, and Mrs. Virginia Moore of near Gladys.

Mrs. J. A. Barnhardt, Keysville, Va. Jan. 18, 1918

Mr. N. I. Walthall has just received a telegram from Parham M. Price announcing the death of his brother, Carrington Price, a soldier at Camp Green, N.C. The remains will be brought to Brookneal for burial tomorrow (Saturday).

Death has visited our neighborhood and taken from us one of our dear friends, Mrs. Emma Wilkerson. She died at the home of Mr. James Brown on the 15th, and was buried on the 16th. She was in her 79th year. She was a worthy woman and had for many years been a member of the Methodist church.

February 1, 1918

Miss Carrie Olivia Hancock, daughter of Mr. and Mrs. J. J. Hancock, died at the home of her sister, Mrs. W. N. Williams, 1821 Carrington St., Richmond, Va., after two days illness of bronchial pneumonia. The body was interred in Mt. Carmel cemetery, Charlotte county, following funeral services conducted in the church by Rev. F. M. Ryburn, of Phenix Presbyterian church.
Besides her parents, Mr. and Mrs. J. J. Hancock, Miss Hancock is survived by four sisters, Mrs. W. N. Williams and Miss Annie Hancock of Richmond and Misses Clara and Edna Hancock, of Phenix, five brothers, J. W., of Richmond, Felix, Peerman, Nathan and Wirt of Phenix.
Dearest Carrie, how we miss you
As the lonely days go by;
You have gone to brighter regions
Safe from every pain and care;
We shall meet again in heaven
And never more be parted there
By L. M. O.

Mrs. Mattie Nash and Mrs. Grace Holcomb have returned to their homes in Lynchburg after attending the funeral of Mr. Carrington Price.

Information was received in Brookneal this week to the effect that Tom Price, an inmate of the Confederate Soldier's Home in

Richmond, died at that institution last Sunday night. He was well known throughout Campbell and Halifax counties.

Aspen-Mrs. Sam Baldwin returned home Monday from Richmond where she attended the burial service of her sister, Miss Sallie Hunt.

Miss Carrie Hancock, of Richmond, daughter of Mr. and Mrs. John Hancock, of Phenix, was buried at Mt. Carmel last Tuesday afternoon.

February 8, 1918

Houston Girl Cremated-Brookneal was shocked to learn of the tragedy which on Monday night overcame the family of Mr. and Mrs. E. S. Lacy of Houston, their 16 year old daughter, Gertrude, being burned to death and their recently occupied $10,000 home being razed to the ground.

Miss Lacy was starting a fire in her bedroom at 7 o'clock with coal oil when her clothing became ignited and in her frantic efforts to unencumber herself of the flaming material ignited the room. The fire quickly communicated with the other parts of the building and pushed by a high wind, it was not long before the house was destroyed.

The injured girl was rescued from the building, but she was so terribly burned that she died a few hours later.

Mr. Lacy is widely known in Halifax county, owning a large hardware store in Houston.

An elder daughter of Mr. Lacy was burned to death about ten years ago.

Mr. and Mrs. J. O. Terry were called to Pamplin Tuesday to attend the funeral of Mr. Terry's brother, Robert, who died Monday.

Miss Temple Cook died at the home of Mr. R. E. Adams last Tuesday morning, aged about 55 years. She was the second daughter of the late William and Nannie Cook and had been an invalid all her life. Her remains were interred in the family burying ground Wednesday afternoon.

Carrington Price, the young soldier, who died at Camp Green, N.C., on January 24th, and was buried here on Sunday, January 27th, was the youngest son of Walter and Viola Price, who preceded him to the grave by several years. He was 27 years old and enlisted in the 31st Infantry August, 1917. His wife, whom he married July 1917, survives him, also one brother, Parham Price, and one sister, Mrs. B. O. Read. The funeral services were conducted in the Baptist church here by Rev. John B. Williams, after which the remains were laid to rest beside his father and mother in the Presbyterian cemetery. The coffin was wrapped in a large U.S. flag and the floral offerings were many and beautiful.

February 15, 1918

Childrey-Mrs. Mary Brown, who has been on the sick list for some time at the home of her sister, Mrs. Dr. Holland, died Sunday morning. She was about a hundred years old.

Stovall-We were sorry to hear of the death of Mr. Billy Murphy. He was buried Sunday in the family burying ground near Clarkton.

February 22,1918

The sudden death of Mrs. W. T. Tribble, which occurred Wednesday night at her home in Halifax county, about three miles from Brookneal, came as a severe shock to her family and the entire neighborhood. Mrs. Tribble appeared well and cheerful and helped her children with their lessons after supper, her death occurring sometime later presumably from heart failure. She is survived by her husband, a well known farmer and several children. Interment took place yesterday afternoon in the family burying ground. Mrs. Tribble was well known in the neighborhood and will be missed by all.

Perth-On Wednesday, February 13th, Mrs. Martha Rice, aged 64 years, died at the home of her son, Mr. J. E. Rice, near here. She had been in bad health for several years, but her death came as a shock to the family. She was greatly loved by all who knew her and she had been a consistent member of the Baptist church for many years. She is survived by her husband, Mr. Joe Rice, and three children, Mrs. J. W. Doss, of Altavista and Messrs. R. C. and J. E. Rice, of this county. She was laid to rest in the family burying ground at the home of Rev. W. I. Hall.

Mr. J. Watts Williams passed peacefully away at his home near Gravel Ridge, Wednesday morning about 9 o'clock, after a lingering illness. Mr. Williams was about 69 years of age. He was a consistent member of New Chapel Baptist Church and enjoyed a wide acquaintance, holding the confidence and esteem of all who knew him. He was noted for his philanthropy and never an appeal for the relief of distress was made to him in vain. In the death of Mr. Williams the Gravel Ridge neighborhood has lost one of its most valuable citizens.

Mr. Williams is survived by six sons as follows: Lafayette, of Philadelphia; Charles, of Concord; John, of Lynchburg; Robert, of Campbell county; Taylor, of North Carolina; George, of Philadelphia, and Tom, now in the United States Military service. Four daughters, Mrs. Dexter Maddox, of Lynchburg; Mrs. Eutaw Maddox, of Mt. Zion; Mrs. Robert Price, of Tweedy's and Miss Mary Williams, of Lynchburg. He also leaves one brother, Rev. John B. Williams of Brookneal, and two sisters, Mrs. M. E. Connely of Gladys, and Mrs. G. A. Bradley, of Lynchburg.

Naruna-Mrs. Susan Monroe died Wednesday, Feb.13. She is survived by her husband and seven children.

March 1,1918

Two Deaths in Gladys-Gladys, Va. Feb.27- Mr. William Farmer died at his home near here Tuesday afternoon after a lingering illness. Mr. Farmer was in his 70th year. The remains were laid to rest at Kedron church cemetery Wednesday afternoon.

Mrs. William Daniel died at her home near this place Tuesday morning. The burial took place at Winfall Wednesday afternoon.

Childrey-We all deeply sympathize with Miss Lona Tribble and the family in the death of her dear mother.

Oakdale-Mrs. Ora Jordan, wife of Mr. Claude Jordan, died at her

51

home at Wren, on February 20th, after an illness of a few weeks. On the afternoon of Feb. 21st the funeral services were held at Midway church conducted by Rev. Mr. Kester, of Red House, assisted by the Rev. G. A. Chocklett and Rev. Frank Cabiness. After the funeral in the presence of a large number of friends and acquaintances, her remains were interred in the cemetery at Midway church. As we write our hearts go out in sympathy to her bereaved husband, mother and father, brothers and sisters.

A little child of Mr. and Mrs. Walter Mason died in a Lynchburg hospital last week. The remains were interred near Naruna.

Naruna-Mr. and Mrs. Lee Robey attended the burial of Mr. Robey's sister, Mrs. Whit Tribble, of Halifax, last Thursday. Rev. A. I. Caudle, of Naruna, preached the funeral of Mrs. Tribble.

Acorn-Several people from this neighborhood attended the funeral of Mr. Richard Gutherie 1st Sunday afternoon in Brookneal.

Mr. Richard A. Guthrie, a pioneer citizen of Brookneal, died in a Lynchburg hospital last Saturday. Mr. Guthrie, who was 61 years of age, had been ill for some time and had been in Richmond and Lynchburg hospitals for treatment. The remains were brought here Saturday evening and interred in the Wickliffe cemetery on Sunday afternoon. The funeral services were largely attended and were conducted by Dr. W. F. Fisher, pastor of the Baptist church. Mr. Guthrie was a native of Halifax county, and was the son of the late Jackson Guthrie. There were seven brothers and one sister, all of whom, with the exception of Mr. J. A. Guthrie, of Halifax county, preceeded him to the grave. He resided in Brookneal for twenty-three years. He had never married but had numerous relatives in Campbell and Halifax counties and was widely known, enjoying the confidence and esteem of a large circle of friends.

MRS. W. T. TRIBBLE-written by the lonely children
On February 20, at 7 o'clock p.m., the death angel visited the home of Mr.W. T. Tribble and claimed his dear wife. She was ill only a short time before death came. Her death was due to heart failure. The funeral was conducted by Rev. A. I. Caudle, of Naruna, in the presence of a large condourse of bereaved relatives

and friends. She was a faithful member of Clover Baptist church, a most devoted mother to her children and a kind neighbor always ready to lend a helping hand. She was laid to rest in the family burying ground. Oh, mama, we hate to give up our loved one. But God makes no mistakes. We will try to meet you in the better home above. We submit to His holy will, but there is a vacant place in our home that can never be filled.

Oh, mama, thou hast left us,
Our hearts are crushed with pain;
But we have a hope that's blessed-
In heaven we'll meet again.
Four lonely days have passed.
We hear your voice no more;
Not even the sound of footsteps
Can we hear ever more
Thou shalt sleep, but not forever
In the lone silent grave;
Blessed be the Lord that taketh
Blessed be the Lord that gave.
We miss you from the table,
There is a vacant chair
We miss you, OH, our loved one
We miss you everywhere.

March 8, 1918

Cody-News was received here on last Tuesday February 26, of the death of W. B. Farmer of Gladys. He was formerly of this neighborhood and had a host of friends who extend to the bereaved family their deepest sympathy.

Following domestic troubles, Mrs. Ethel Walton, aged twenty-six, wife of S. J. Walton, of Windsor, committed suicide by sending a bullet through her heart. The woman attempted to end her life by drinking crude carbolic acid, but a doctor from Ivy relieved her of the poison. The fatal bullet was fired during the temporary absence from the room of her husband. Mrs. Walton was a Miss Coleman, of Albemarle, and was married nine years ago. Five children survive, the youngest being only two months.

Died on the night of February 25, at his home at Cedar Forest, Pittsylvania county. Mr. R. Bascom Carr, in the 68th year of his age. He had been in bad health for some time though death came unexpected. He leaves a wife and six children, three sisters and one brother together with a host of friends to mourn his death. The funeral services were conducted by Rev. W. L. Mays, of the M. S. E. church. The remains were laid to rest in the family burying ground.

We were sorry to learn of the sudden and sad death of Mrs. Ellen Hubbard, who died Thursday night, Feb. 28. She was laid to rest Saturday at the home place of Mr. Tom Worsham. Rev. T. J. Hudson conducted the funeral services.

March 15, 1918

Terryville-Mr. Andrew Smith died last Friday and was buried in the family cemetery Sunday afternoon.

Mount Zion-In the death of Mr. J. Watt Williams the community has suffered a serious loss. He will be greatly missed in the church and in the prayer meetings. He was a kind neighbor and a great hand to visit the sick. He left his children a blessed heritage in the example he set before them.

Aspen-Mr. T. N. Gaines who has been in bad health for several years died last Thursday afternoon at his home near here. He was buried in the family cemetery at Mr. Joe Gaines'.

March 22, 1918

Philip Epes, a respected and faithful colored citizen, who was noted for his honesty and square dealing, also for his unobtrusive and inoffensive character, died yesterday morning. Philip will be missed by both white and colored.

Miss Zelia Thomas, 18 years old, youngest daughter of Mr. and Mrs. A. F. Thomas, of Lynchburg, died at the Lynchburg hospital Wednesday night, at 8 o'clock, following an operation Monday for appendicitis.
Besides her parents she is survived by the following brothers and

sisters; Gallitan, Willard and Alsen Thomas and Misses Vera, Marie and Eustacia Thomas , all of Lynchburg.
Her brother Willard enlisted in the navy Monday and left Tuesday night for Norfolk.

Mr. W. B. Farmer, who lived two miles from Gladys, departed this life February 26th. He was 70 years old the 17th of last December. The greater part of his life was spent in Pittsylvania and Halifax counties. Mr. and Mrs. Farmer were blessed with a happy family of ten children, all living. They were exceedingly watchful concerning the children's highest interest, especially their education and their company.
Mr. Farmer was enthusiastic about the improvement of public roads, public schools, churches, etc. He was an interesting talker and an inspiring listener. Mr. Farmer was above the average man in point of intelligence.
At the time of his death he was an honored member of Kedron Baptist church and as active as his declining years would permit. He was interested in all departments of christian activity. He remarked during the wet and dry campaign if 1914 that he would be willing to die when Virginia goes dry. He knew some time before the end came that he could not get well. He watched for the setting sun. As the shades began to thicken about him he spoke calmly of his passing over and made several requests about his grave and also requested that mourning would not be worn.
Mr. Farmer is survived by his wife and following children: Mrs. Thomas, Gladys; Mrs. Davis, North Carolina; Mrs. Davis, Washington; Dr. Harvey Farmer, Richmond; Manly Farmer and Mrs. John Edmonds, Glays; Walter Farmer, Alaska; Mrs. Giles Nichols, Allen Farmer and Ruth Farmer, Gladys.

March 29, 1918

Card of Thanks-Mr. W. L. Lash and family wish to express their sincere and heartfelt thanks to the good people of Brookneal for the many kindnesses shown them in their recent bereavement.

George Lash, aged 22 years, was the third son of Mr. and Mrs. W. L. Lash, of Brookneal. He was a private in Co. L 317th Infantry, at Camp Leg. His death which resulted from pneumonia, occurred last Thursday at about 11:30. The remains were brought here Friday evening and interred in the family burial lot in the Wickliffe cemetery Saturday at 1 o'clock. The funeral services were conducted at the home of the deceased by Rev. W. F. Fisher, pastor of the Baptist church, and the burial took place under the auspices of the Odd Fellows, of which the deceased was a member. Members of the order acted as pallbearers, and the floral offerings which were many and beautiful were borne by fourteen young ladies.

Mr. Lash is survived by his father and mother, three sisters and three brothers as follows, Msses. Katy, Lucy and Gertrude, and Messrs. Frank and Louis, of Brookneal, and Chapman, of Hopewell.

On the evening of March 14, 1918, the death angel called and took from Mr. and Mrs. J. W. Stevens their son, John Will, aged 18 years old.

He was accidentally hurt the day before while playing a game of baseball with the school children. He was hurried to a hospital in South Boston, where he lived only a few short hours.

Only a few months before he had enlisted as a volunteer in the Coast Artillery to serve his country's cause.

He was a popular young man of Republican Grove neighborhood and was liked by all who knew him.

He leaves mother, father, four brothers, one sister and a host of friends and relatives to mourn his death.

He answered to the call of his country, but the Lord knew what was best. So he was called for a Heavenly purpose, and now with the angels he'll rest. R. L. Burton

"Aunt Dinah" Young, a widely known colored woman, died at the home of her son-in-law, Henry Scott, in Halifax, last Sunday morning.

Resolutions of Respect-In memory of Brother George Lash, who died March 21st, 1918.
So, let him sleep that dreamless sleep;
Our sorrows clustering 'round his head;
Be comforted, ye loved who weep.
He lives with God-he is not dead.

****

Oddfellowship:
Working in manhood's prime and ardent youth
In that subilmest, most enobling strife,
To show for man, best Friendship, Love and Truth.
Green be his memory in the Order's heart
He loved so well, through all his true life's span;
Bless'd be his rest, who acted well his part,
Who honored God in doing good to man.
****

Once again death hath summoned a Brother Odd Fellow, and the golden gateway to the Eternal city has opened to welcome him to his home. He has completed his work in ministering to the wants of the afflicted, in shedding light into darkened souls and bringing joy into places of misery, and as reward has received the plaudit "well done" from the Supreme Master.

And, Whereas, the all-wise and merciful Master of the universe has called our beloved and respected brother home, and he having been a true and faithful member of our beloved Order, therefore be it

Resolved That Brookneal Lodge No. 267, I.O.O.F., of Brookneal, Va., in testimony of her loss, be draped in mourning for thirty days and that we tender to the family of our deceased brother our sincere condolence in their deep affliction, and that a copy of these resolutions be sent to the family, a copy spread upon the minutes of our Lodge and a copy sent to the Union Star for publication.

T. O. Myers
W. R. Walker
W. H. Ginther, Committee

Andrew Lewis Spurr, seventy seven years old, and so far as known the last surviving member of the famous old Stonewall Brigade Band, was taken ill suddenly at his home in Winchester a few days ago, and is in a serious condition.

In Memorium-Whereas, it has pleased our Heavenly Father in His all-wise and overruling providence to remove on January 7, 1918, from our community to a higher sphere, our beloved sister, Mrs. Fannie Brooks, who from the beginning of our Union has labored with increasing interest.

And whereas, while being submissive to divine will, which is perfect love, we desire to place on record our consciousness of loss and our sincere appreciation for her faithful service well rendered;

Therefore be it resolved, That we, the Woman's Missionary Union of Kedron Baptist church, Gladys, Va., give unto God our thanks for the long life and constant service of our sister, whose interest and sympathy with us was always helpful and ended only with her "home going." We shall miss her presence, for she was faithful in attendance, always on time, thus manifesting her interest in the welfare of the Union;

That we express to the family our heartfelt sympathy with them in the glorious hope which is theirs in Christ Jesus, realizing that our loss is her eternal gain;

That a page of the record of the Union be inscribed to the memory of our departed sister, that a copy of these resolutions be sent to the bereaved family and a copy sent to the county papers for publication.

Respectfully submitted,
Mrs. L. D. Morgan
Mrs. Will Morgan
Mrs. G. S. Thomas
Mrs. Nathan Pugh

Seneca-Mrs. S. F. Armstrong is expecting to leave for Hagerstown, Md. this week. She has been with her sister since the death of her niece, Jeane B. Ware.

The people of this neighborhood were shocked by the death of Jeane Bell Ware who fell from the bridge across Seneca creek and was drowned. We extend our heartfelt sympathy to the bereaved mother and family.

April 12, 1918

Dies at Camp Lee-The body of Jacob Hoy Kline, son of J. F. Kline, of Gladys, was brought there Monday morning from Camp Lee, where Mr. Kline died Sunday morning of pneumonia. The burial took place Tuesday afternoon at 3 o'clock at Wesleyberry church. Besides his father and several brothers and sisters, Mr.

Kline is survived by his wife, who was Miss Estelle Danill. They were married last fall.

April 19, 1918

Mrs. Mattie Harvey, wife of Mr. Wyatt Harvey, of near Hat Creek, died at her home Wednesday afternoon after a lingering illness. Interment took place Thursday afternoon.

Mr. Jake Kline, who had been in training at Camp Lee, was buried at Wesleybury M.E. church April 10. We extend our deepest sympathy to the family.

April 26, 1918

David T. Elder, a well known farmer, died at his home near Brookneal last Saturday after a lingering illness. Interment was made near the home on Sunday afternoon in the presence of a large gathering of friends of the deceased and the sorrowing family. In the absence of a minister the services were conducted by B. F. Ginther.

Mr. Elder was in his 66th year, having been born in July, 1852. He resided among the people of this community all his life and they had learned to love him. He was of a quiet and unobtrusive disposition, of industrious habits and a good citizen who will be missed by the entire community. He is survived by his wife and six children, the oldest of whom is Curtis C. Elder, aged about 22 years old. The bereaved family have the heartfelt sympathy of the entire community.

Mrs. A. M. Moon spent Sunday night in the home of Mr. W. A. Mason en route to her home at Hopewell, after attending the funeral of Mrs. W. W. Harvey.

The funeral of Mrs. Mattie Harvey who died at her home near Hat Creek Wednesday of last week, was conducted on Thursday afternoon by Rev. J. A. Scott, after which interment took place in the Presbyterian cemetery. Mrs. Harvey is survived by her husband, Mr. W.W. Harvey; five children as follows, Corporal Henry Lee Foster, of Camp Lee, Hilton, Welford and Mabel

Foster and Elizabeth Harvey; also one brother, Mr. R. A. Reynolds.

Card of Thanks-We wish to extend to the good neighbors and friends our sincere and heartfelt thanks for the many kindnesses shown us during our recent sad bereavement in the death of our husband and father.
Mrs. Emma L. Elder and Family

May 3, 1918

In Memoriam-In sad but loving remembrance of my dear husband, David T. Elder, who departed this life April 20th, 1918. All that physicians, friends and loved ones could do was done, but none could stay the cold hand of death. It was God's appointed time to take him to a better world where death and sorrows are unknown. He was a kind and loving husband and father. He had been a member of he Baptist church the greater part of his life and was a member of the Brookneal Baptist church at the time of his death.
Thou art gone, dearest husband,
Thy mission has been filled,
Thy smiles we do remember,
If death thy voice has stilled.

Dearest husband, thou hast left us.
Left us yes forever more,
But again we hope to meet thee
On that bright and happy shore.
Thou art gone, dearest husband
Thy crown of life is won;
Thou wilt be missed dearest husband,
Oh, yes, by more than one.
Fare thee well, dearest husband,
On earth we'll meet no more,
But thou art free from storm and pain
On that eternal shore.
By his devoted wife, Emma L. Elder

May 3, 1918

Childrey-Mr. Dick Jennings quite an old man, died on the 20th and was buried near Ellis Creek on the 21st. He will be greatly missed by a large circle of friends and relatives.

May 10, 1918

This community was shocked by the untimely death of Mr. Alfred Bently who shot himself last Monday morning. Interment was made at Sharon graveyard Tuesday.

Mr. W. P. Scott died at the home of his daughter, Mrs. John Roakes, Friday morning and was buried at Kedron church Saturday. We extend our deepest sympathy to the family.

May 17, 1918

Former Naruna Boy Drowned at Richmond-Richmond-May 13-Edward G. Evans, a ministerial student at Richmond College, from Texas, a sophomore, was drowned in the lake at an early hour this morning. Mr. Evans was in the habit for the last several weeks of donning his bathing suit and going down to the pond. He went out this morning, and when he failed to return at the usual hour his friends because uneasy and began to make a search for him. They went to the edge of the lake and saw where he had entered the water. Students began to drag the lake, the body was found and brought to shore.
Mr. Evans was born and raised near Naruna. For several years he had made his home at Deer Lake, Texas, to which place his parents had moved. His body was taken to Texas for burial.
****
A memorial service will be held in Edge church (of which Mr. Evans was a former member) next Sunday afternoon at 3:30 o'clock.

May 10, 1918

Mrs. Allen Tweedy died suddenly at her home near Rustburg
Tuesday afternoon. Interment was made in the New Chapel
Baptist church burying ground.

Mr. James Bohannon died at the home of his daughter, Mrs. J.M.
Smith, Tuesday at 4 o'clock, after an illness of brief duration. The
deceased had lived all his life near Abell at which place the
remains were interred Wednesday. Rev. J. E. Davis, of the
Methodist church, conducting the services.

Mrs. Ora Bessie Hurt, widow of T. W. Hurt, died Saturday at the
home of her sister, Mrs. R. O. Elder, near Brookneal. She is
survived by two children, Lucile and Owen, her father J. R.
Harper, and the following brother and sisters, J. D., E. J., N. T., R.
H., Will and T. P. Harper, Mmes. W. A. Ferris, R. O. Elder, B. H.
Watkins and B. L. Coffey.

On Monday afternoon there was laid to rest the remains of the late
Pleasant R. Walker, one of the last survivors of his company,
which was one of Campbell's companies in the Confederate army.
He was born in the Goose Creek Valley of Bedford County
November 8, 1829, and had he lived until Thursday of this present
week, he would have celebrated the 58th anniversary of his
marriage with Miss Sallie Patrick.
He was a lifelong member of the Baptist Church, an honored
citizen of the county, and much loved by the whole community.
The services were conducted by the Rev. W. L. Jones. His sons
were the honorary pallbearers and his granddaughters were the
flower bearers.

Card of Thanks-Mr. Editor: Please let us express our appreciation
to our friends and neighbors for the kindness and sympathy
rendered us in the illness and death of our sister, Mrs. Bessie Hurt.
Mr. and Mrs. R. O. Elder

May 17, 1918

The burial of Mr. J. M. Webb, who died last Saturday morning at 11:20 o'clock, after a lingering illness, took place Sunday afternoon at 2o'clock in the Wickliffe cemetery.
Mr. Webb was born November 10th 1839 in Appomattox county, being in his 79th year at the time of his death. He served in the war between the states form 1861-1865 in Co. H 2nd Virginia Calvary. Mr. Webb is survived by his wife, two daughters and two sons, Mr. J. E. Webb, of the Webb-Adams Hardware Co., Misses Effie and Ella Webb, of Brookneal and Mr. Tom Webb, of Richmond. Services were conducted by Rev. W. F. Fisher.

On April 31 Mrs. George E. Roby, of Halifax county, died at her home near Perth. All that loving hands could do was done to keep her with us, but God saw fit to take her away. She had been ill only 3 weeks before her death.
She is survived by her husband, George E. Roby, and three children, Elvey, Grace, and Ozell; also her father and mother, Mr. and Mrs. Willis Clay, and four brothers, Dick, John, Boss and Jesse Clay, and one sister Mrs. Wright, all of Halifax county.

Card of Thanks-We desire to express our sincere thanks to the good people of Brookneal for the many kindnesses shown us in our sad bereavement.
Mrs. Grace J. Webb and family

Mrs. Allen Tweedy, nee Miss Trixy Coates, died suddenly last Tuesday, the 7th, at the home of her father, Mr. Walter Coates, near Mount Zion. It has cast a gloom over the neighborhood. She was 17 years old and had been married but four months. Trixy was greatly loved by all who knew her and as I looked upon her in her coffin shrouded in her wedding attire with the bridal wreath resting upon her marble brow I thought of the lines of the poet: "Joy, however unstained by sorrow, and hope, however glad, must find an end in death." She is survived by her husband besides her parents, two brothers and two sisters: Mr. Willie Coates, of Mount Zion; Mr. Clarence Coates, of Fortress Monroe; Mrs. Thornton, of New Chapel and Mrs. Claytor, of Mount Zion. Her family are almost broken-hearted and we deeply feel for the young husband in his great sorrow.

Her remains were interred in the Tweedy burying ground near New Chapel church. The funeral was conducted by Rev. P. O. Soyars, of Gladys. His text was taken from the 14th chapter of John. We pray that God will comfort the hearts of her loved ones and let them remember that they have a hope of meeting her in a better land.

Mrs. Cheatham

May 24, 1918

In Memoriam-In loving remembrance of our friend and coworker. God in his infinite wisdom has seen fit to take from our midst and Missionary Society, Mrs. Wyatt Harvey.

In her death the society sustains that the loss of one of our good members, who was faithful to the work and whose death casts a gloom over the society.

Twas in the home of her life was most beautiful always encouraging her loved ones to all that was pure and holy, thus leaving them a rich heritage by precept and example.

To the bereaved ones we extend our heartfelt sympathy and commend the to the God of all comfort.

Resolved that this memorial be spread upon our minutes and a copy be sent to the family.

Pres. Mrs. J. S. Scott
Vice Pres. Miss Cassie Clark
Treas. Mrs. Wirt Williams
Sec. Mrs. L. C. Asher

In MEMORIAN-Mosby Rice died April 20th near Gladys, Va.
He laid down in manhood's prime,
A bright young form and brave.
Which gaunt disease with fatal hand
Had grappled for the grave.
Kindly faces bent above
The stricken dear boy's bed
And loving hands the pillow smoothed
That held his dying hand.
For loving ministration did
His mother's hand employ;

Sister and brothers too were there
To serve their much loved boy.
Those loving hands their pity gave
And gentle eyes their tears
For one whom death had conquered in
The springtime of the year.
And where Virginia's skies are bright
Virginia's mountains hoar
Spread their mantling shadow broad
The smiling landscape o'er.
They made his grave a sunny spot
Upon a hillside fair,
Where birds and butterflies will love
To drink the summer air.
On a sunny morning bright,
At noonday's peaceful hour,
With reverend hand they laid to rest
Their cherished well-loved flower.
A Friend

June 14, 1918

Oakdale (Charlotte County)-Mr. and Mrs. Thornton Covington
lost their little six year old daughter in a horrible manner last
Sunday. The child was in the house by herself and in some way
her clothing caught fire and she ran out of the doors and before her
parents could get to her she burned to death.

June 21, 1918

Hat Creek-Mrs. Juda Johnson died June 7, at 10 o'clock a.m. She
was 67 years old. She was buried in the family grave yard. Dr.
Scott preached the funeral.

July 5, 1918

Cole's Ferry-Miss Leady Mason died a few days since after a
lingering illness. She was the daughter of Mr. and Mrs. E.G.
Mason. Her parents, four sisters and four brothers survive her.
Deceased was nineteen years of age and leaves a host of friends.

July 12, 1918

The body of Wayland Kersey, seventeen years old, who died of peritonitis following an operation for appendicitis at a hospital in South Boston, Monday, was brought to Brookneal Tuesday, and taken in charge by Jere White & Co's undertaking department and conveyed to his home at Aspen for burial. He was the son of Tom Kersey.

Randolph-Mrs. Woodson Berkley was buried last Wednesday at Bon Air. Mrs. Berkley was before her marriage Miss Emma Jackson, of this county, and her friends are grieved to know of her death.

Mrs. Jeff Lipscomb died at her home the 18th and was burried (buried) the 20th in the family cemetery.

July 19, 1918

The seven year old child of Mitchell Elam, colored, died at its home near Terryville last Saturday and was buried Sunday. The child had been afflicted all its life.

Fred Clowdis, son of Mr. Woody Clowdis, of near Abell, was accidentally killed at Akron, Ohio, on Saturday, July 13. The remains were brought home and interred at Mt. Carmel Wednesday afternoon, Rev. J. E. Davis, the pastor, officiating. Mr. Clowdis is survived by his father, mother and three brothers, Hugh, Frank and Harold, all of whom reside near Abell.

The funeral of the late John W. Cabaniss took place Sunday, July 14, from Greystone, the residence of his brother, Capt. Wm. G. Cabaniss, where early Saturday morning he passed away into his eternal rest.
He was in his 68th year, and beside his brother, Capt. Wm. G. Cabaniss, leaves a number of nephews and nieces, having lived a bachelor all his life.
The interment was made in Hat Creek cemetery, conducted by Rev. A. K. Lambdin. The hymns "There's a Land That is Fairer

Than Day," and "Jesus Lover of My Soul" were sang. Those attending from a distance were Rev. F. G. Cabaniss, of Clover, Mr. E. A. Cabaniss, of Roanoke, and Lieut. Marvin Cabaniss, of Philadelphia, Pa.

Mr. W. A. Jones who has for many years been a resident of the neighborhood, passed away at his home July 12. He had been ill only a few hours and the news of his death came as a shock to his many friends. The funeral services were conducted by his pastor, Rev. P. O. Soyars, assisted by Rev. John B. Williams, in Kedron Baptist Church, of which he had been a faithful member for a number of years. A large crowd of his neighbors and friends filled the church and followed the remains to the last resting place in the church cemetery. Rev. John B. Williams sang, "Death is Only a Dream," Nearer My God to Thee," "Asleep in Jesus," "Shall We Meet," and "In the Sweet By and By" were sung in the church and "Day is Dying," "Jesus Lover of my Soul," and "How Firm a Foundation" were sung at the grave. Mr. Jones is survived by his wife and nine children, Mrs. Lee Winston, of St. Louis, Mo.; Mrs. Gaskill of Atlantic City, N.J., Miss Lillian Jones of Charlottesville, Va.; Mrs. Goggin, Mrs. Will Blanks, Rev. J. S. Jones, Messrs. Willie and Mike Jones and Miss Ira Jones, all of Gladys and a number of brothers, sisters and grandchildren. To the many relatives and friends, we extend our deepest sympathy and pray God's love and care may comfort them in their bereavement.

July 26, 1918

Mount Zion-We are grieved to hear of the death of Mr. Button Jones. The family has the deepest sympathy of this neighborhood in their trouble.

August 9, 1918

In Memoriam-Men's Bible class of Kedron S.S.
Whereas. It has pleased "the Great Commander" to call our brother, William A. Jones, from his earthly toils and cares, to his heavenly rest. Be it resolved
That in the sudden death of Brother Jones the community has sustained the loss of one of its esteemed citizens and generous

neighbors, his pastor a loyal friend, the church and Sunday school a zealous number and his family an amiable, cheery and devoted companion and father.

And in recognition of his virtues, his years of patient toil sufferings and sacrifices, his generous disposition, loyalty as a friend and a churchman and his labors of love, we desire to express and place upon record some measure of appreciation and the esteem of his hosts friends for his long life and unselfish career.

Also to extend to the members of his bereaved family and to his friends sympathy at his sudden departure and in the hour of their sorrow to commend each of them to the love and mercy of the God upon whom he relied and in whom he trusted; and to admonish each of them to strive to enter into that rest that remaineth to the people of God.

That a copy of these resolutions be spread upon the minutes of the Church, a copy given to his family and a copy sent to each of our county papers for publications.

"There is no death, the stars go down
Only to shine upon some fairer shore,
And bright in heaven's jeweled crown
They shine, shine forever more.
"There is no death, the leaves may fall
And flowers may fade and fade away,
They only wait through wintry hours
The coming of new light and life and day.
"There is no death, an angel's spirit or form
Walks through the earth with silent tread;
He bears our best loved things away
And we call them dead.
"Borne into that undying life
They leave us, but to come again;
With joy we welcome them the same
Freed from their sin, their toil and their pain.
"And ever near us, though unseen,
The dear immortal spirits tread;
For all the boundless universe
Is life-there are no dead."

Mrs. Willie Reynolds, wife of Mr. Jim Reynolds, died at her home in the border of Halifax county about 2 o'clock Wednesday morning, aged 40 years. She had been ill for several weeks with a complication of diseases. She was the eldest child of the late John Reynolds, of Campbell county, and besides her husband and little daughter she is survived by her mother, one brother and three sisters. She had for many years been a member of Falling Baptist church and her remains were interred there Wednesday afternoon. Mrs. Reynolds was a good woman and a kind neighbor and had many friends in her circle of acquaintances.

August 16, 1918

In Memoriam-On Wednesday morning, August 7, about 1 o'clock the death angel visited the home of Mr. Jim Reynolds, in Halifax county and took from him his beloved wife, Mary Willie. All that loving hands could do to save her was done, but God knew best and took her to rest. She had been ill for several weeks but her death came as a shock to her many friends and relatives. She had been a member of Falling Baptist church and her remains were interred in the cemetery there Wednesday afternoon.
She was the eldest child of Mr. and Mrs. John Reynolds, Campbell county. She leaves to mourn her loss, her husband, Mr. Jim Reynolds, and one little daughter, Frances; three sisters, Mrs. Sam Rylie, Mrs. Munk Cyrus and Mrs. Evens Liftige, all of Campbell county; and one brother, Mr. Johnnie Reynolds, of Cullen, also her mother, Mrs. Fannie Reynolds, of Campbell county, and many friends.

Holly Plain-Mr. William Harper died last Thursday and buried at Beulah church last Friday. Rev. W. F. Fisher, the pastor, conducting the funeral. The family has our sympathy.

Staightstone-We were sorry to hear of the death of little Reed Motomer. We extend to Mr. and Mrs. Motomer our deepest sympathy.

Mrs. Emily S. Jennings died at her home, Clifton, Charlotte county, August 7, 1918, aged 89 years. She is survived by three children, Mrs. Chas. Rudder, of Charlotte county, C. S. Jennings, of Campbell county, and Mrs. Mattie Shaner, of Illinois. She has twenty grandchildren and eight great grandchildren.

The pall bearers were John Owen Frank Mason, George Wade, Scott Mann, Meade Holt, George Wallace and Gordon Lipscomb. The flower bearers were Misses Lizzie and Ethel Mann, Alma Hamlett, Mary and Copeland Mason.

August 23, 1918

Republican Grove-Mrs. Cindy Hill, aged 99 years, died at the home of her daughter, Mrs. Dick Duncan on the 6th of August.

Mr. John Fisher died at his home near Volens on the 8th day of August.

August 30, 1918

Sudden Death-Mr. Thomas F. Williams died Friday morning at 9:15 o'clock at the Williams House after an illness of a few minutes from acute indigestion. Hew was complaining before breakfast but ate and went back to his room where he called for relief in a few minutes. Two doctors were called and everything was done that was possible.

Mr. Williams is survived by his wife and five children who live at Chase City.

Mr. Williams has been for about twenty years with the Virginia Carolina Chemical Company.

Friends from Chase City arrived in the afternoon to take charge of the remains which were conveyed back to his home on the evening train.

The death of Mrs. Cabell Carrington Scott took place at her home here Tuesday afternoon after an illness of several months.

Before her marriage she was Miss Mary Pringle, daughter of the late Captain William Goode Pringle, of Brookneal.

Mrs. Scott was a member of the Brookneal Baptist church which she joined early in life.

She is survived by her husband, one daughter, Miss Cornelia Scott, and one sister and two brothers ; Mrs. Pendleton Emmett and R.B. Pringle, of Lynchburg and John Pringle of Washington.

Her funeral took place at the residence Wednesday afternoon and interments was made in the old Calloway cemetery.

September 6, 1918

Childrey-Our hearts were made quite sad on Saturday, the 24th, to learn of the death of Mrs. Leola Puckette Rudder, who was taken to a Lynchburg hospital about ten days preceding her death. She was tenderly laid to rest near her home in the presence of many sorrrowing friends and relatives. Her death was a shock to all. Only a few Sundays before her death the writer had the sweet privilege of hearing her teach her class in Clover Bottom Church, in which she was a devoted member as well as teacher. She has five daughters and three sons, Mrs. Edward Guthrie, Mrs. Sedie Blanks, Mrs. Laban DeJarnette, Misses Inez and Flossie Rudder, and Messrs Tommie, Lewis and Carroll Rudder to mourn her death besides a large circle of relatives and friends.
We deeply sympathize with the family of Mrs. Will Rudder in the death of her husband, which occurred in a Lynchburg hospital last Thursday night and whose remains were bought to their old home near Martin's store Saturday for interment. May God's richest blessing rest with this family in their sad hour.

Melrose
Mrs. J. T. Rudder, who died after an operation in a Lynchburg hospital, was buried at her home Sunday afternoon. She was of a most lovable character and will be greatly missed, especially in the Sunday school where she was a regular attendant.

Card of Thanks-We wish to express our thanks and appreciation to the good people of Brookneal and also of Halifax county for their many kindnesses and expressions of sympathy during the illness, death and burial of husband and father, William T. Rudder.
Mrs. W. T. Rudder and family

September 13, 1918

Randolph-We were sorry to hear of the death of Morris Payne. He was killed in action on July 29th somewhere in France.

September 20, 1918

News was received here yesterday of the death of Miss Mae Brewer, of Richmond, her parents, Mr. and Mrs. S. N. Brewer, were formerly of this place.

Mr. Edd Harvey has received a telegram announcing the death of his brother, Mr. Walter Harvey, who left in the first call last fall for Camp Lee. He did not stay there long before he was transferred to Camp Green. He made his trip across early in 1918 and was wounded in July and died of his wounds.

September 27, 1918

Abell-Mr. Willie Johnson received a telegram last Friday announcing the death of his adopted son, Private Martin Johnson, who joined the army in Sept. 1916, in West Va. and went from there to do guard duty on the Mexican border. Later he went to Camp Shelby, Miss., and from there to Camp Merrit, N.J., from whence he sailed to France. Where was a member of Co. B. 166th Infantry when he was killed in action on the 28th of July.

Oakdale(Campbell County)-Mr. Lee Howard has returned home from Richmond where he attended the burial of his niece, Miss May Brewer.

Naruna-Mrs. A. H. Pugh has received a message announcing her death of her brother, Private R. L. Kesler, son of Mr. and Mrs. W. H. Kesler, of Madison Heights. Private Kesler was killed in action in France on August 8th. He was drafted in Amherst county Sept. 18, 1917, and was trained at Camp Lee. He was a member of Co. M, 38th Infantry at the time of his death.

October 4, 1918

Brookneal was shocked and saddened Tuesday by the news of the death of Mr. Stephen M. Clay, a former citizen of this place, which occurred at his home in Charlottesville on Monday, from paralysis. Mr. Clay had been in Brookneal on business only a few days before his death and was looking unusually well. He was a native of Campbell county, being born on June 30th, 1854, and was entering his sixty-fifth year. He is survived by his wife and three children. Mrs. Clay was Miss Ada Courtney Mallory, Ashland. The children are Courtney M.. Mrs. J. E. Webb and Mrs. S. B. Jones. Interment was made in Richmond Wednesday.

Perth-Our neighborhood was shocked and saddened last Friday evening when it was learned the Mr. Geo. Layne had been found dead, his death having been caused by an accidental gunshot wound inflicted while squirrel hunting Friday morning. Mr. Layne is survived by his wife and four children. He was well known and popular, having a host of friends. The remains were interred in Clover Bottom cemetery. The funeral services being conducted by Rev. Mr. Barbour.

October 18, 1918

Shirley O. Dunn died at his home in Halifax county, near Brookneal, last Saturday after a short illness from pneumonia following an attack of influenza. The remains were brought to Brookneal for burial Sunday afternoon. Mr. Dunn was 46 years of age and leaves a wife and five small children.

Courtney, second son of Mr. and Mrs. J. H. Williamson, of Spring Mills neighborhood, died in Lynchburg on Wednesday, Oct. 9th, of influenza. The remains were brought home and interred in Diamond Hill cemetery. The obituary notice written by Mr. S. H. Williamson is necessarily omitted on account of its length and our inability to do composition under present circumstances explained elsewhere in this paper.

Naruna-This community was shocked by the sudden death of the 2-year-old child of Mr. and Mrs. John Pool, who died last Thursday.

Card of Thanks-Mrs. S. O. Dunn and children wish to thank the public generally for the many kindnesses shown on the occasion of the death and burial of their beloved husband and father, Shirley O. Dunn.

We were deeply grieved to learn of the death of Rev. P. O. Soyars, of Gladys, who was known and loved by many of the Crosby people.

October 25, 1918

Naruna-Mrs. Pearl Helen Carwile, wife of Private Luther Carwile, died last week in a hospital at Petersburg from influenza. She was laid to rest at Sharon Methodist church. The parents have the sympathy of the entire neighborhood.

In Memoriam-Whereas, Our Heavenly Father, in His wise providence, has seen fit to remove from his earthly toils to his Heavenly rest our loved pastor Rev. P. O. Soyars, we the members of the W.M.U. of Kedron Baptist church do earnestly desire to place on record some word of appreciation for his faithful service during the two and a half years he has been our pastor.
"How beautiful are the feet of those that reach the gospel of peace, and bring glad tidings of good things." His chief delight was to preach the gospel of peace, and bring glad tidings. He was ever on the watch and never let an opportunity pass of telling others of Christ.
His loved ones have lost a kind, tender and loving husband and father the church, a faithful pastor, our society a wise and zealous counselor and worker, the young people and children a tender, devoted instructor and guide and the community a sympathetic friend and neighbor.
His cheery presence, his ever ready smile, his hearty handshake, and his genial personality will long be remembered and sadly missed.
We well remember his last talk at our Missionary meeting, when he urged the true missionary spirit, the spirit of gift, not money only, but loving deeds, of personal work among those of our community who could not meet with us, with the shut-in and all whom we could cheer and brighten with song and prayer.
Although his place is vacant and cannot be filled, his life among us has left its impress upon our church and the surrounding community.
When we think of the need of such as he, of the work he had done, was doing and had planned to do, of the aged parents, the wife and children crushed and broken-hearted, we wonder at his going, going too in the vigor and strength of manhood, with his large

views, of the privileges that lay before him, and yet, God makes no mistakes, and with this thought in our minds we shall endeavor to go on with our Master's work, looking, as our pastor did, continually to Him for strength and leading.

We keenly feel our sorrow and loss, yet we do not sorrow alone. Our church and our community share in mourning.

Therefore be it resolved:

First-That we bow in humble submission to a loving Master who doeth all things well.

Secondly-That we extend to the aged parents, the bereaved wife and children and to the many loved ones and friends our deepest sympathy and commend them to a loving Father who hurts only for our good.

Third-That a copy of these resolutions be sent the family, a copy placed on the records of our society and a copy sent to the county papers for publication.

Miss Annie Connelly
Mrs. G. R. Nichols
Mrs. L. D. Morgan
Mrs. E. S. Webb

November 1, 1918

Gladys-Miss Lena Miles, of Lynchburg, and Mrs. Edward Miles, of Gladys, were buried at Kedron cemetery last Sunday at twilight. The funeral services were conducted by Rev. J. S. Jones, Rev. A. W. Roten, both of Gladys and Rev. Jackson of Fairview Heights.

November 8, 1918

Mrs. Mary Smith Berkley, wife of Mr. Jas. G. Berkley, of near Naruna, died Wednesday morning at the home of her daughter, Mrs. A. H. Hawkins, in Lynchburg. She is survived by her husband and two daughters, Mrs. A. H. Hawkins, of Lynchburg, and Mrs. W. E. Collins, of South Boston, and five sons, Geo. and James, of Naruna; Robert , of Fort Washington, Md; Wheeler and Thomas, who are in the service overseas. She is also survived by five sisters and two brothers. Her body was taken to Naruna for burial.

Mrs. Lizzie Morton died in the home of Mrs. C. W. Tibbs and was laid to rest at Sharon church. She was a member of Ebenezer church. Mrs. Morton left a husband and two children.

November 8, 1918

Mrs. A. H. Pugh has received many letters expressing sympathy for the death of her daughter, Mrs. Pearl Carwile.

Mr. Andrew Morton has returned to Danville after the death and burial of his wife.

Mrs. W. O. Tune left Tuesday morning for Richmond to take her brother-in-law's children to him. They had been here since the death of their mother a few weeks ago.

Mr. Richard Dalton, of Phenix, wishes to thank the good people of Brookneal for their kindness during the illness and death of his sister, Mrs. Little, and for notifying him of the circumstances; also for the many nice flowers.

November 15, 1918

Mr. John Daulton, of Chalklevel, Pittsylvania county, droped dead last Wednesday night, death being due to heart failure.
He is survived by his wife and seven children and the following brothers and sisters, C. J. Daulton, of Gladys; Ell and Alice, of Pittsylvania county and Mrs. Wallace, of Halifax county. He was buried in the family burying ground near Cedar Forest.

The neighborhood was greatly shocked to learn of the accidental death of Mr. George E. Roby, caused by being struck by an automobile driven by Pete White, of Brookneal, son of Mr. Jere White. Only last spring he lost his wife, who was Miss Mary Lou Clay before her marriage. She left three little girls, Evelyn, Gracie and Ozelle. Mr. Roby was married the second time only one week before his death to Mrs. Joe Guthrie. He lived only about two hours after being struck. He was buried by the Woodman in the family burying ground near Volens. The family wishes to thank the neighborhood for the many kindness shown in their bereavement.

Death Calls Suddenly-Lynchburg-John Bell Winfree, Sr., one of the oldest residents of Lynchburg, who for many years was a successful tobacconist until he retired from business, and who though probably seventy was identified with the interests of the Methodist Church, died Sunday at his residence on Federal Street. Mr. Winfree had been ill about twenty-four hours, and his death was due to angina pectoris.

Bristol Man Killed in France-Bristol-Paul Massey, another Bristol boy, was killed on the front according to news received by relatives. He was a member of Company H, One Hundred and Seventeenth Infantry. He had formerly served on the border during the Mexican trouble.

November 22, 1918

Mr. C. E. Monroe, aged 58 died at the home of Mr. A. R. Elder last Thursday at 7 o'clock. He was buried Friday at the G. D. Elder burying ground. He had been in a hospital in Norfolk for several weeks but was discharged and came home here where he took a relapse. His death was attributed to pneumonia following influenza.

A Note of Thanks-It is with deep appreciation that I received and read the sweet comforting letters and messages from friends from all over Virginia and other states since the death of my dear husband which occurred on October the 10th.
I take this opportunity of expressing my sincere thanks to his many friends for the beautiful expressions regarding his life, and the comforting words to his family. I also wish to say that his family has not been forgotten by his faithful flock since he was taken from them.
We have been remembered in many ways by both the churches, Kedron and Winfall.
Friends and neighbors of other denominations have been exceedingly kind to us. For All this we are very thankful.
Mrs. P. O. Soyars. Gladys, Va.

November 29, 1918

Card Of Thanks-Mr. and Mrs. S. M. Childress wish to extend their sincere thanks to the many good people of the neighborhood for the many kindnesses and sympathy during the illness and death of their little child.

December 6, 1918

Mr. Dorsie Jordan died in the Lynchburg hospital Monday night. We have great sympathy for his people.

December 13, 1918

Naruna-We were sorry to hear of Mrs. Jennie Sublett's death.

Mr. Dan Sublett died Dec., 9th, and was buried at Sharon church Dec. 10th.

Our community was very much saddened by the death of Dorsey Jordan, only 18 years of age. He had an attack of the flu, followed by an abscess in his head from which blood poison set in. The end came Tuesday night of last week at 9 o'clock in the Lynchburg hospital. He leaves a father, mother, one sister and a number of brothers. The family has our deepest sympathy.

December 20, 1918

C. W. Elder, age 29, died at his home near Crosby Wednesday night of influenza. The remains are to be interred at Falling church today. Mr. Elder is a son of Mr. Wesley Elder and leaves a wife and three small children.

Miss Lula Davidson, 19 years old of Mr. and Mrs. S. W. Davidson, died at her home near Crosby Wednesday evening as a result of pneumonia following influenza. Miss Davidson is survived by her father, mother, two sisters and three brothers. Interment was made at Falling church at three p.m. yesterday, the funeral services being conducted by her pastor, Dr. W. F. Fisher.

Buried at Naruna-Lena Virginia, twenty years old, daughter of Mr. and Mrs. L. P. Valley, died at her home on 1221 Pierce St., Lynchburg, Wednesday morning, Dec. 4 at 4 o'clock after an illness of several months. She was a member of College Hill Baptist church and a consecrated christian. She is survived by her parents, two brothers, Napoleon and Joe, four sisters, Marie, Beatrice, Myrtle and Evelyn, and a host of friends to mourn her departure. The funeral took place at Ebenezer Baptist church, at Naruna, on Thursday, Dec. 5th. Services were conducted by Rev. A. I. Caudle. The pall bearers were S. C. Holland, W. E. Sowell, Dewey Sowell, C. H. Dalton, Robert Nash, and J. T. Pollard. The flowers were carried by Mrs. Daisy Maddox, Mrs. Pency Childress, Misses Gracie Hunter, Lizzie Elder, Ida May Elder and Lula Sowell.

Mrs. Napoleon Angel died at her home near Brookneal Tuesday morning as a result of influenza. The remains were taken to Clover Bottom, Halifax County, Wednesday, for burial. Mrs. Angel is survived by her husband and several children, all grown. She was about sixty years of age.

Gertrude, the little daughter of Mr. and Mrs. B. F. Richardson, died at the home of her grandparents, Mr. and Mrs. W. H. Jackson, last Saturday of influenza. The funeral services were conducted by Rev. J. B. Williams.

Card of Thanks-We wish to thank the kind people in Brookneal for their sympathy, attention and assistance during the illness, death and burial of our little daughter, Gertrude. Especially do we wish to thank the following gentleman for their kindness: Messrs. B. B. Cox, W. J. Coleman, W. T. Wright, Conway, Frank and Mitchell Guthrie, Richard Snell, Paul Elder, Stafford Bates, H. B. Barksdale and Sam Saunders.
Mr. and Mrs. B. F. Richardson

Mrs. H. E. Stevens died at her home at Crosby last Saturday morning and was buried at Falling church on Sunday. She is survived by her husband and two children. Her death was caused by influenza.

December 27, 1918

Miss Thelma Walker received a telegram from Richmond last week announcing the death of her uncle, Mr. Bernard Johnson, who had been ill for some time.

Miss Katie Mason received a message this morning stating that Miss Maude Moon died last night at her home in Lynchburg.

This neighborhood was saddened by the death of Hamilton, the little son of Mr. and Mrs. W. W. Jordan, of Seneca. His death was caused by influenza.

Mmes. L. D. Harvey and S. E. Crafton were called to Charlotte C.H., last Tuesday on account of the death of their sister, Mrs. Littie Williams, who died of influenza at her home there on Monday. They returned home on Wednesday only to be called back again yesterday by the death of their mother, Mrs. T. S. Carey, which occurred on Christmas Day. Mrs. Williams was about 32 years of age and is survived by her husband, Mr. A. S. Williams, and two children. Mrs. Carey was 65 years if age and is survived by her husband and two daughters, Mmes. Harvey and Crafton, and one son Jas. T. Carey of Keysville.

On December 18,1918, the death angel entered the home of Mr. and Mrs. S. W. Davidson and bore away a loving daughter and sister, Lula Christine. A dark shadow is now cast o'er us; there is a vacant place at the table, and around the fireside circle. There is a vacant place in the Sunday school class and amongst the young people's gatherings. Our meetings seem incomplete without her. We miss her, O! so much. She was ever ready and willing to help someone. She was indeed popular amongst both old and young. But we must all remember that she is not dead but asleep. "A deep sleep from which none can e'er wake to weep."
Lula was in her nineteenth year and a more promising church member and Sunday school worker would be indeed hard to find. She had been an active member of Falling River Baptist church from early childhood, at which place she was laid to rest on Thursday, Dec., 19th. The pall bearers were Messrs. Willie and Whitney Asher, Edward Marshall, Johnny Davidson, Luther Elder

and Willie P. Holt. Services were conducted by her pastor, Rev. W. F. Fisher. Besides her parents, she is survived by two sisters, Maude and Mary and three brothers, Charlie, Everett and Jesse. N. G. H.

Our community was saddened by the death of Mrs. W. A. Mason last Sunday morning. Her death was due to double pneumonia. She had been a faithful member of Diamond Hill Presbyterian church for years. She was laid to rest in the family burying ground Monday evening. She will be greatly missed.

A sad death occurred in Brookneal last Saturday morning when Mrs. Bettie Daniel, wife of our well-known townsman, Mr. Joe Daniel, passed away. Mrs. Daniel's death was due to diabetes from which she had been suffering for some time. She was in her 30th year, and was well liked by all who knew her. Besides her husband and little son, Walter, she is survived by her father and mother, Mr. and Mrs. R. L. Mays, of Lynchburg, one sister and four brothers, one of whom is in France. The remains were taken to Lynchburg for interment.

Card of Thanks-We desire to express our sincere and heartfelt thanks to the many good people Brookneal who were so kind and considerate and rendered such valuable assistance during the illness and death of our beloved daughter, Mrs. J. W. Daniel. Most especially do we wish to mention Mr. O. S. Stephens for his tireless attention and service.

January 3, 1919

Card of Thanks-We wish to express our sincere thanks to the kind neighbors and friends of Charlotte and Campbell counties for their interest and assistance during the recent illness and subsequent death of Mr. C. W. Elder and wife.
H. N. ELDER

January 10, 1919

Our community was very much saddened by the death of Mrs. Pless Worsham, who died at the home of her daughter at Seneca, her little grandson having died a few days before with flu.

Gladys-Mr. Dewey Ritcherson died with double pneumonia following flu.

Mrs. C. J. Daulton is dead after ten months of suffering. She is survived by her husband and the following children: Mrs. Lee Robey and Mrs. Lacey Woolridge, of Naruna, Mr. C. H. Daulton, of Gladys, Mrs. Morton, of Lynchburg, John Letcher Daulton, of France, Carlton Daulton and one adopted daughter, Rubie Newman, and one brother, Mr. G. G. McHaney, of Gladys. She had been a member of Kedron church for the past seventeen years. She was laid to rest at Kedron New Year's day. Rev. Mr. Ayers conducted the burial services.

January 17, 1919

Rustburg, Jan. 14-Alphonzo F. Hancock died at the home of his brother, W. T. Hancock, Saturday morning of pneumonia following influenza. He is survived by his mother, Mrs. P. P. Joy, of Spring Mills, and one brother W. T. Hancock, and one sister, Mrs. J. H. Rucker, of Rustburg. Interment was at New Chapel church, and the funeral services were conducted by Rev. J. M. W. Elder, of Concord.

Death of Estimable Colored Woman-Lucy Smith, wife of James Smith, died last Saturday of pneumonia, on the premises of Mr. W. D. Ramsey, where they have lived for the past ten years. She was buried Sunday afternoon at Nazarene church, Charlotte county, of which she was a member. She will be greatly missed by many of the white people as well as the colored. She leaves a husband and eight children.

January 24, 1919

In Memoriam-Emory Atkins, age 25, killed by gas in action in France.
We have lost our darling brother,
He has bid us all adieu;
He has gone to live in Heaven,
And his form is lost to view.
Oh, that dear one, how we loved him!
Oh how hard to give him up!
But an angel came down for him
And removed him from our flock.
Farewell, dear father, brothers, sister,
Weary with years and worn with pain,
Farewell, till in some happy place
We shall behold thy face again.
'Tis ours to miss thee, all our years
And tender memories of thee keep;
Thine in the Lord to rest-
He giveth his beloved one sleep.
We miss thee from our home, dear brother,
We miss thee from thy place,
A shadow o'er our life is cast;
We miss the sunshine of your face;
We miss the kind and willing hand,
Thy fond and earnest care,
Our house is dark without you-
We miss you everywhere.
Weep not that his toils are over,
Weep not that his race is run,
God grant we may rest calmly,
When our work, like his, is done.
'Till then we yield with gladness,
Our Father to him to keep,
And rejoice in the sweet assurance,

"God giveth His loved one sleep."

Charlotte C.H.-Mrs. E. F. Smith died on the 16th of January and was buried at Midway on Saturday. May the good Lord comfort those left to mourn.

We all feel very sorry for Mr. Albert Tuck. The flu has claimed four out of his family. May the Lord comfort the bereaved family. Mrs. Hitchie Dunn died of pneumonia. She leaves a devoted husband and eight children to mourn for her. We pray for God's blessings to abide with them all.

Mr. and Mrs. Kinder lost their baby last week. The little one had suffered very much since having influenza. It was taken to Tazewell for burial.

Abell-We were both surprised and sad to hear of the death of Mr. Thompson Crews, a prominent young man of Halifax county. Mr. Crews died with pneumonia following an attack of influenza. The community has lost one of its best citizens. He will be greatly missed both in the home and community.

The community was saddened and shocked by the death of Mr. Herbert Moon, who died Jan. 7th. His death was due to the flu.

Mr. Whit Short, of near this place, died recently. His death was caused by the flu. The family have the deepest sympathy of the community.

Oakdale (Charlotte County)-This neighborhood was shocked to hear of the death of Mrs. Richard Sublett, who lived near Jordan's Gate.

Naruna-There have been several deaths from influenza among the colored people of Naruna.

January 31, 1919

Rev. H. H. Farris and wife-These two good people left their home at Church Road in Dinwiddie county, where they moved into the

Baptist parsonage, the first of November to take charge of two strong country churches, to visit Mrs. Farris' people it Lynchburg during the Christmas holidays, arriving there with their dear child nineteen months old December 24th, all three in good health.

On Christmas evening Mrs. Farris was stricken with influenza. In a few days she developed a serious case of pneumonia and on the last day of the historic year 1918, she went to be with the Lord whom she loved and served.

Brother Farris was taken with the same disease a few days after his wife. On the day that she died, against the advice of his loved ones and friends, he would get out of bed, being in distress, although he had a mild case of the disease, and walking the floor and in the hall-way. However, he did not attend the burial of his companion the 2nd day of January because of the fact that he was worse, and in a day or two also went into pneumonia and died on the morning of the tenth of January, 1919. Both were laid to rest in a Lynchburg cemetery to await the second coming of our Lord and Saviour, Jesus Christ.

This preacher of the dear Saviour was a son of Mr. and Mrs. Manson Farris, of Gladys, Campbell county, Virginia, and died at the early age of 24 years and his wife 23 years. Brother Farris was educated in the public schools of Virginia, Chatham Training school, Fork Union Military Academy and Richmond College. In July, 1916, he was happily married to Miss Martha Smith, daughter of Mr. and Mrs. K. H. Smith, of Lynchburg, who spend the winter months in that city and the months of the summer on ther (their) large plantation down on the James river in Appomattox Co. Brother Farris went out from Kedron church at Gladys while the writer was pastor there, he being ordained there two and a half years ago. He was pastor of the Meherrin field of three churches for three years and did the best work there since the organization of those churches, and they had some strong men who preceded him in the work above mentioned. He was a fine preacher, a good pastor, much beloved by his people. I have been living in close touch with him for three years and I know of his earnest labors. If he had lived he would have made a preacher that any church might be proud of. He had already led many souls to the Saviour in the pastorate and in special meetings. Farewell, my brother, until we meet in the Father's home.

J. A. Barnhardt, Keysville, Va., Jan. 18, 1919

Mrs. W. D. Colbert died at her home in Lynchburg, Jan. 20. Her death was caused by pneumonia following influenza. Mrs. Colbert is survived by her husband and four small children, also her father and mother, J. H. and Elvira Lee, of Lynchburg, one brother, J. W. Lee, of Milwaukee, Wis., and four sisters, Mrs. Elsie Wingfield, of Lexington; Mrs. W. H. Pillow, Brookneal; Mrs. Bessie Creasy, Lynchburg, and Mrs. C. R. Carwyle, Naruna.

The flower bearers were Mrs. W. T. Hancock, Mrs. Blance Hancock, Mrs. Pattie Sandifer, Mrs. Mason, Mrs. Maddox and Mrs. Morris.

"Jesus Saviour, Pilot Me," and "Sweet Peace" were the hymns sung at the house and "Sleep on the Beloved" at the grave by a quartet from Court Street Methodist church.

She was laid to rest in the Spring Hill cemetery Wednesday afternoon.

Mrs. Colbert was loved by all who knew her and will be greatly missed by her many friends and relatives.

"He was called for many a loved one,
We have seen them leave our side;
With our Saviour we shall meet them,
When we, too, have crossed the tide.
When we have passed the vale of shadows,
With its dark and chilling tide,
In that bright and glorious city
We shall evermore abide."

Death has thrown its dark shadow across the threshold of another home. A beautiful flower has been plucked from the garden of earth, to be placed in the brighter realms of heaven.

On the 20th of December, at Brookneal Campbell county, Virginia, Bettie Mays Daniel, the beloved wife of J. W. Daniels, in her 31st year, entered the Kingdom of Heaven. In the morning of life, bright, joyous, dutiful, affectionate and loved by all who knew her. Equally lovely in person, character and faith, this pure soul passed from earth. Her short pilgrimage was marked by the brightest Christian graces, unselfish devotion to husband, father, mother, brothers, sisters and friends, a scrupulous regard for the comfort, happiness and welfare of others, and a forgetfulness of self, as rare as it is beautiful in life. A faithful friend, and a bright example has been lost to the community. A dutiful daughter, a warmhearted, affectionate sister to a devoted family. Yet amid all this gloom comes a silver lining to the black cloud of despair and heart crushing anguish that follows such a loss. Her pure unselfish character is an example to those who must follow. The cheerful voice is no longer heard in the grief stricken home. The splendid example of Christian virtues yet remain to console the bereaved hearts that mourn their loss. To save others may have been her mission on earth. She was a member of the Methodist church, and leaves a husband, one son, mother, father, four brothers and one sister to mourn her loss.

"Leaves have their time to fall,
And flowers to wither at the Northwind's breath;
And stars to set-but all-
Thou hast all seasons for thine own, O Death!"- One who knew her well.

The Saltville correspondent of the Lynchburg News announces the death of, Rev. John R. Mathews, which occurred there on the 22nd inst. of pneumonia following influenza.

Mr. Mathews was an Episcopal minister and was known and loved by many in this section, he having conducted several mission services, at Clarkton.

He was born and reared in Manchester, England and was an A.M., of Oxford University. He came to this country about twenty years ago and took up the mission work of his church, holding mission services all over this and other states. Last fall he settled in Saltville, where he has doubtless done the crowning work of his life. Soon after his arrival, the influenza epidemic broke out and his work was great. He kept going day and half the night, visiting every home he could possibly reach, ministering with peculiar tenderness and sympathy to spiritual and material needs of the suffering.

Bear Creek-Doyal, the small son of Mr. and Mrs. Walter Wright died Wednesday afternoon, January 15th, from pneumonia following an attack of influenza.

February 7, 1919

Mrs. S. C. Hubbard died February the 2nd at 9:45 a.m., and was buried February the 3rd at 2 p.m., at her home Springwood, Halifax County. Funeral services were conducted by Rev. J. B. Lavinder of Brookneal. The pall bearers were her six sons. Her oldest grandchildren, Kathleen and Mamie Rosser and Herbert and Richard Hubbard bore a blanket of flowers which completely covered her grave. The other flower bearers were Mamie Hubbard, Lucy LaPrade, May McIvor, Carrie Davis, Flossie Rudder and Alice Davis. Mrs. Hubbard was a member of St. John's Episcopal Church, Houston, VA. She was before marriage, Miss Anna Carrington, of Halifax. She was seventy-two years of age the 21st of January and had been married fifty-one years, Oct. 30, 1918. She had been an invalid for fifteen years but bore every moment of her suffering patiently. She is survived by her husband, S. C. Hubbard, two daughters, Janie and Anna and six sons, E. Carrington, Samuel C. Jr., Robert M., J. William, and E. Randolph, all of Halifax, and Clem R., of Lynchburg, one sister, Mrs. Eliza Moon and one brother, E. M. Carrington, of Charlotte County, also fifteen grandchildren.

Our community was immeasurably shocked Monday night by the announcement that Mrs. Lillie Rush, wife of Lacey W. Rush, had died suddenly. She was in her usual apparently robust health until about 3 o'clock Monday afternoon when she was taken suddenly ill. Medical aid was summonded, but she became unconscious in about an hour and despite all that could be done for her relief she expired about 9 o'clock, death being due to apoplexy. Mrs. Rush was in the 45th year of her age and was a daughter of the late Dr. G. M. Wickliffe. She joined the Baptist church in her girlhood and has since remained a loyal and consistent member. She was a kind neighbor, a stauch friend, a faithful wife and a most devoted mother.
She is survived by her mother, Mrs. Mary J. Wickliffe, her husband and nine children. The funeral services were conducted at the residence Tuesday afternoon by her pastor, Rev. W.F. Fisher,

assisted by Rev. J.
B. Lavinder, of the Methodist church, and Rev. John B. Williams,
after which her remains were interred in the Wickliffe cemetery.
Her popularity was attested by the lage (large) numbers who
attended the obsequies notwithstanding the inclement weather.

February 14, 1919

The funeral of Mrs. W. S. Elliotte, who died in a Lynchburg
hospital some time ago will be held at Hat Creek on Saturday, Feb.
15th at 12 o'clock. The body has been held in a vault in Lynchburg
pending the recovery of Mr. Elliotte.

On the morning of Feb. 11th, 1919 the death angel came to the
home of Mr. and Mrs. Houston Tanner and took their darling
baby, Walter Hugh, age one year and one month. He died of
pneumonia after a few hours of suffering. He was laid to rest near
his home Friday afternoon about 4 o'clock. He leaves to mourn a
father and mother and one little sister.

February 21, 1919

We were sorry to hear of the death of Neal, son of Mr. Tom Lee
Foster, which occurred last Saturday. He was buried at Union Hill
Sunday.

Card of Thanks-Mr. and Mrs. W. S. Carwyle wish to thank the
many good people of their neighborhood for the attention rendered
them during the illness and death of their mother, Mrs. Lucy A.
Tibbs, who departed this life on Feb. 11th.

The body of Mrs. Ethel Roden Elliott, aged 35, wife of W. S.
Elliott, who died December 21, 1918, in a Lynchburg hospital of
influenza, was laid to rest Saturday at 1 o'clock in the Hat Creek
cemetery. The services were conducted by Rev. Thorton Wilson,
of Halifax, assisted by Dr. Scott, of Hat Creek.
The pall bearers were: Messrs. George Marshall, Lewis Asher, M.
Bailey, N. Harper, of Hat Creek, and R. D. Williams and Dr. W.
O. Tune, of Brookneal.
Misses Asher and Lawson and Mrs. Kenneth Henderson and Mrs.

Carwile were flower bearers. A number of Brookneal friends attended the funeral.

Mr. and Mrs. Harold Torrence, of Plum Branch, paid a short visit to latter's parents, Mr. and Mrs. Rice Carwile, Sunday afternoon. Mr. Torrence's grandfather, Mr. Socrates Haden, is very ill, suffering from a wound inflicted during the Civil War.

Mrs. Tibbs, aged 76, died at the home of her daughter, Mrs. N. S. Carwile, near Kew, a few days ago. The remains were laid to rest at Falling church. She is survived by one daughter, Mrs. Martha Carwile, of Kew, and two sons, Robert Tibbs of Kew, and Richard of Naruna.

February 28, 1919

New Bethel-Mrs. Pierce Carwile died at her home near here Saturday morning of influenza. She leaves her husband, two sons, William and Arthur, two little daughters, Ethel and Margaret, ill with influenza and another daughter, Lizzie, very ill with consumption. The funeral services were held at her home by Rev. J.W. Marsh, of Concord, and her remains were carried to her old home church Wesleybury at Gladys. The services were concluded at the grave by Rev. A.
W. Roten, assisted by Rev. D. G. Trent and Saunders Jones. She was laid to rest in the presence of a large number of friends. Only two members of the family, Ruby and Reese were able to attend the burial. The family have the sympathy of the entire community.

The whole community was shocked to hear of the death of Mrs. Pierce Carwile, Feb. 22. She is survived by her husband and seven children. She was laid to rest at Wesleybury church Monday at 3 o'clock.

March 7, 1919

In Memorian-In true remembrance of our dear mother who departed this life one year ago, Feb. 20, 1918.
From this world of grief and trouble
To the land of peace and rest

God has taken our dear mother,
There to find eternal rest.
Tenderly we cared for her
Trying to restore her health;
Prayed that she might longer stay,
Which to us meant more than wealth.
Now the mid-night stars are beaming
Upon her lone and silent grave,
Where she slumbers without dreaming-
The one we tried in vain to save.
'Tis so sweet to be remembered,
And a pleasant thing to find
Although she's forever absent,
She is ever on out mind.
Written by her daughter, Lona Tribble.

March 21, 1919

Mrs. Roxana Monroe, daughter of the late Llewlyn and Martha
Elder, departed this life Sunday morning, March 9, 1919. The
deceased was sixty years old and had been a consistent member of
the Baptist church since early girlhood. Although shadows had
crossed her married life she had a brave and cheery welcome for
the numerous friends and relatives who loved to visit her home.
Her remains were laid to rest in Ebenezer cemetery where her
father, mother and son are resting. The presence of a host of
relatives and friends, as well as the beautiful floral offerings attest
the deep love and esteem that all had for her. Six of her brothers
acted as pall bearers and her nieces carried the flowers. The
funeral services were conducted by her pastor, Rev. A. I. Caudle.
She leaves eight children to mourn her loss, whose names are as
follows: Messrs. Bunyan, Roy and Pelham Monroe, of Gladys, her
daughters are, Mrs. Nowlin Elder, of Brookneal, Misses Nannie,
Grace, Lucy and Maggie Monroe. The latter two are teachers,
Miss Nannie is a stenographer in Beckley, W.Va., and Grace is a
stenographer in Lynchburg. Her brothers are J.W. and S. B. Elder,
of Brookneal, R.F.D., Robt. Lee Elder, of Naruna, Henry
Sylvester, Geo. W. and C. O. Elder, of Gladys. Her sisters are Mrs.
I. B. Suddith, of Gladys, Mrs. Emma Mason, of Brookneal, Mrs.
C. W. Hunter and Mrs. B. E. Pool, of Naruna.

Sister thou wast mild and lovely,
Gentle as the summer breeze,
Pleasant as the air of evening,
When it floats among the trees."
"Peaceful be thy silent slumber,
Peaceful in the grave so low,
Thou no more shalt join our number
Thou no more our song shall know."
"Yet again we hope to meet thee,
When the day of life is fled.
Then in Heaven with joy to greet thee
Where no farewell tear is shed."
Her sister

March 28, 1919

Aspen-Mrs. Florence Mason, daughter of the late William and Ella
Hamlette, died Friday, March 21st, 1919. The deceased was 35
years of age. She had been a consistent member of the Baptist
church since early girlhood. Although shadows had crossed her
life, she had a brave and cheerful welcome for numerous relatives
who loved to visit her home. Her remains were laid to rest in
Staunton river cemetery, where her three children rest. The
presence of a host of relatives and friends, as well as the beautiful
floral offerings attested the high esteem and love which we all had
for her. The funeral services were conducted by Mr. W. T.
Claybrooks. She leaves a husband and seven children to mourn her
loss.

On the 7th day of March 1919, Brother Robert Carwile was called
to his reward from his home at Naruna, Va. He was seventy-eight
years old and had been a faithful and consistent member of the
Ebenezer Baptist church for forty-eight years. He was zealous in
the Master's work, and until four years ago when he was stricken
with disease, was a regular attendant at all services of his church.
He was a patient sufferer and bore his pain without a murmur. A
loving wife and five devoted children survive. Messrs. C. H. and
A. R. Carwile, of Naruna, Misses Annie and Cassie, of Lynchburg
and Miss Ollie, of Naruna. The remains were laid to rest in the
family burying ground in the presence of a host of sorrowing

friends and loved ones. The funeral services were conducted by his pastor, Rev. A. I. Caudle. "Blessed are the dead who die in the Lord." May the Lord comfort the bereaved ones. His Pastor

April 4, 1919

Charles W. Harvey, a well known citizen of Brookneal, died suddenly Saturday afternoon, his death being attributed to heart failure. Mr. Harvey, who made his home with his sister, Mrs. W. L. Williams, went out to look after some pigs. Failing to return to the house in a reasonable time, members of the family went to see what was detaining him and found his lifeless body at the barnyard gate. He was 62 years of age and was a native of Charlotte county, and unmarried. The remains were taken to Charlotte county for interment Monday at about 11 o'clock. Mr. Harvey is survived by three sisters, Mmes. I. M. Smith, of Lynchburg, and Mrs. W. L. Williams and R. F. Connally, of Brookneal, and one brother, Mr. W. C. Harvey, of Lynchburg.

Mr. Charles O. Scott, one of the best known farmers of the Naruna neighborhood, died about noon last Saturday following a stroke of paralysis. Mr. Scott had been in poor health for a number of years. The funeral services were held Sunday afternoon at Ebenezer Baptist church, of which the deceased was a member, and were conducted by his pastor, Rev. A. I. Caudle, assisted by Rev. John B. Williams. Mr. Scott was about 65 years of age and is survived by his wife and a number of children, all grown. In the death of Mr. Scott the community has just lost a valuable public spirited citizen.

April 18, 1919

R. R. Cumbie, a prominent farmer of near Rustburg committed suicide last Monday by shooting himself three times. Mr. Cumbie had been in bad health for some time and his mind is thought to have become slightly unbalanced by his affliction. He was a brother of L. C. Cumbie, of Rustburg, and was in advanced years. His wife had gone to the pasture to attend to some stock and upon her return found his lifeless form in the floor.

Mrs. W. D. Price was buried at Kedron cemetery last Tuesday. The funeral services were conducted by Rev. A. I. Caudle, of Naruna, Rev. J. A. Barnhardt, of Keysville, and Rev. Mr. Kesler, of Red House. Mrs. Price was known and loved by almost everyone in this section.

April 25, 1919

Mr. Charles McDowell, of near Brookneal, recently received official information of the death of his son, Private Guy McDowell of the 7th cavalry, in France on March 7th, of spinal meningitis. Private McDowell, previous to entering the service of his country was a student for the ministry in Richmond College. A letter from F. W. Boatwright, president of the college to Mr. McDowell, under date of April 7th, says," I heard with sincere sorrow of the death of your son, Guy. So far as I know he was the first student of Richmond College to volunteer after the United States entered the war. When it was suggested to him that he might await developments, he said that he had thought the matter over thoroughly and felt that it was his duty to go. I had sincere appreciation for your son's worth as a man and a Christian. He was deeply in earnest about preparing for his life's work and he felt that he had a mission to serve his fellow man. He leaves a good name at Richmond College and we shall cherish his memory." A letter was also received by Private McDowell's mother from his chaplain in France, speaking in the highest terms of praise of her deceased son.

May 16, 1919

Deputy Sheriff S. C. Henderson and sergeant L.L. Tucker were called Sunday night to arrest Jim Tucker, colored, for felonious assault on Edgar Bacon, another negro. The officers found Tucker at his home, heavily armed with two large revolvers. When the announced their presence and demanded that Tucker come out and surrender himself he refused and as officer Henderson attempted to open the door Tucker opened fire on him. Mr. Henderson returned the fire with the result that Tucker was wounded three times from which he died early Monday morning in a Lynchburg hospital to which he had been rushed for surgical aid. The deputy sheriff was exhonerated at a preliminary hearing presided over by Mayor B. F. Ginther and justices J. E. Peterson and J. E. Uzzle. Both Negroes were intoxicated at the time of the trouble and a pint whiskey flask was found in Tucker's possession a little more that half emptied.

May 23, 1919

Frazer Thornton Abbot-On the night of May 15, 1919, the death angel entered the home of Mr. and Mrs. J. T. Abbot and took away their little daughter, Frazer. She was one year and 20 days old and a bright little one., but God wanted her to shine for Him. Weep not, dear parents and loved ones, for she has gone to join the happy band of angels, where she will never know sorrow or suffering again. 'Tis hard to give her up but our loss is her eternal gain. May heaven seem nearer and dearer to us and let us strive harder to meet her there. Her remains were carefully laid to rest in the family burying ground. The burial services were conducted by Mr. Johnnie Stevens. The songs "Nearer My God to Thee" and "Safe in the Arms of Jesus" were beautifully rendered. The pallbearers were Messrs. Ranold Waller, Willie Foster, Wesley Arthur and Dick Duncan. The flower bearers were Misses Annie Waller, Ada Belle Long, Anna Fisher, Lillie Long, Annie Stevens and Carlyle Long. She is survived by her parents and two sisters who have our deepest sympathy in their bereavement. The floral offerings were many and beautiful.

Naruna-Mrs. Eva Sowell, who was so severly burned a few weeks ago died last Tuesday. The burial was held at Sharon church Wednesday. The services were conducted by Rev. A I. Caudle and Rev. Mr. Kesler.

May 30, 1919

Mrs. Agnes Williams, daughter of the late Charlie and Mandy McKiney, died May 13, 1919. The deceased was 25 years of age. She had been a consistent member of the Baptist church since early girlhood. Although shadows had crossed her life she had a brave and cheerful welcome for numerous relatives who loved to visit her home. Her remains were laid to rest in Staunton River cemetery. The presence of a host of relatives and friends, as well as beautiful floral offerings attested the high esteem and love which we all had for her. The funeral service were conducted by Mr. Charlie Holt. She leaves a husband and two children to mourn her loss.

Mr. G. R. Nichols died Saturday at 8 p.m., after a long illness. He was buried at the family grave-yard Sunday at 6:30 p.m. Mr. Nichols was much loved and will be sadly missed in this community. He is survived by his wife, two sons, Messrs. Giles and Harvey Nichols, two daughters, Mrs. Sam Dinwiddie and Mrs. Emmett Harris, one brother, Mr. W. E. Nichols and many grandchildren and other relatives. We extend our deepest sympathy to the family.

June 6, 1919

Mr. Charles Moorman Clay, of Brookneal, who for the past three years has made his home with his daughter, Mrs. D. H. Cardwell, died Friday evening at 8:12. The deceased was born in Halifax county, March 27, 1842, was a Confederate veteran and after the war devoted his time to farming and merchandising. He is survived by the following children: Mrs. D. H. Cardwell, Brookneal, Mrs. C. L. Howard and Miss Bert Clay, of Greensboro, N.C., Misses Dossie Mary and Nettie Clay, of Washington, D.C., James M. and Whit G. Clay, of Campbell county, J. Fisher Clay, of Newport News, and Charlie T. Clay, of the 80th division, who has just returned from overseas; one brother James D. Clay, of Halifax county, and two sisters Mrs. Mary A. Burruss, of Lynchburg, and Mrs. Lizzie Shotwell, of Halifax county. Interment was in the family burying ground Sunday, June 1st, at 3:30 p.m. Services were conducted by Rev. W. F. Fisher, of Brookneal, and Rev. Roten, of Gladys. The pallbearers were his four sons, his son-in-law, D.H. Cardwell and grandson, D. H. Cardwell, Jr., of Brookneal.
Flower bearers were Mrs. E. T. Yeaman, Mrs. L. F. W. Clay, Misses Dora and Annie Moore, Minnie Perrow, Erie and Maggie Hunter and Eva Fitch.
His popularity was attested by the large number who attended the obsequies and the many beautiful floral tributes.

On Monday morning, April 19th, the death angel visited the home of Mrs. W. R. Holland, of Ellett, Montgomery county, Va. and bore away the sweet spirit of her mother, Mrs. Mary Edness DeJarnette, after an illness of only a short time of pneumonia following influenza. All that loving hands and kind physicians could do was done, but of no avail. She has had quite a number of severe cases if illness during the past few years, but she bore them patiently and often said she didn't fear death, and was ready to go when her call came.

She was about fifty years of age. She was very active in Sabbath school and missionary work and was always present if her health would permit. She was a faithful wife, devoted mother, loyal to her church, society and pastor, kind and loving neighbor.

The remains were brought to her old home near Childrey and laid to rest in the family burying ground on Easter Sunday by her husband who preceded her to the grave quite a number of years ago. The burial services were conducted by her old pastor, Rev. J. H. Bass, in the presence of a large concourse of sorrowing friends. The flowers which loved ones tenderly placed over her last resting place were not more pure than was her life. Mrs. DeJarnette was the daughter of Mr. and Mrs. James F. Guthrie. She leaves to mourn her death one daughter, Mrs. Mamie O. Holland and several grandchildren and many friends.

Spring Mills-The death angel came into our midst last Monday and took from Mr. and Mrs. F. H. Lee, their darling little infant only a few weeks old. Our hearts go out in sympathy to the bereaved parents.

Died at his home at Gladys, Va., May 24th, 1919, Mr. G. R. Nichols, aged sixty seven years. He had been a great sufferer for a number of years from diabetes, and for the past six months, was confined to his bed, which trial he bore with meekness and patiently awaited the end.

The funeral service was held at his late home on Sunday afternoon, in the presence of a large congregation of friends and neighbors, conducted by Rev. J. A. Barnhardt, of Keysville, Va., after which, his remains were laid to rest in the family burial ground near by, where repose the ashes of his sainted father and mother and other loved ones.

Mr. Nichols was a member of the Methodist Protestant church, which organization he joined many years ago. He was prominent in the community in which he resided and served his county faithfully for a number of years, in the capacity of constable, assistant treasurer and road commissioner. Perhaps, no man, throughout the county was a stronger advocate of good roads than he, and to this end he exerted his efforts, so far as his power lay. It was his disposition to enter heart and soul in to any and everything which he undertook and many were the sacrifices he made for others, even to his own detriment at times. He was a loyal husband, devoted father, generous friend and true neighbor, and will be sadly missed in his home, community and large circle of friends and acquaintances.

Mr. Nichols is survived by his wife, she was Miss Nannie Bailey before marriage; also by two sons and two daughters, who are as follows; Mr. Harvey Nichols and Mrs. Emmett Harris, of Lynchburg; Mrs. Samuel Dinwiddie and Mr. Giles Nichols, of Gladys. He also leaves a number of grandchildren and one brother, Mr. William Nichols, of Roanoke. To each of these bereaved ones, our hearts go out in profound sympathy, and ask God's grace may prove a sufficiency for them in these trying experiences of life.

Since he is gone, know there is no death,
An angel comes and lifts the soul of faith.
In joyous ecstacy unto our God,
While we are left to pass beneath His rod.
Mrs. J. S. Barnhardt, Keysville, Va., May 31, 1919

June 13, 1919

Mr. Jerry McCulloch, an old and well known citizen of Halifax county, died at his home in the border of Halifax near Brookneal Sunday morning, June 8th, after a lingering illness from paralysis, in the 84th year of his age.

Mr. McCulloch had been a member of the Baptist church for more than fifty years and enjoyed the respect and confidence of his neighbors. He was the father of seven children, one of whom died in childhood and is survived by his widow, three sons and three daughters.

His remains were interred in the family burying ground Monday afternoon in the presence of a large number of friends and neighbors., the service being conducted by Rev. W. F. Fisher. The flower bearers were all his grand-daughters.

Boy Drowns in James-Lynchburg-Thomas Edward Morris, fifteen year old son of T. J. Morris, was drowned in the James River here. The lad went to the river with a lot of Sunday school mates and waded out into the river. Stepping in a hole over his head his companions thought he was playing and discovered too late that he was drowning. Half an hour dragging recovered the body.

June 20, 1919

We were very sorry indeed to hear of the death of Mr. and Mrs. Boss Ingram's little baby boy who died Friday and was buried Saturday afternoon. It had been ill for some time.

Mike-Mr. T. A. Canada and little daughters, Marie, Garnet and Mildred and Mr. Samuel Williamson motored to Halifax last Saturday and attended the burial of Mr. and Mrs. Bass Ingram's little son, Randolph, their only child. We extend our deepest sympathy to the bereaved family.

June 27, 1919

Mr. G. W. Foster, seventy-four years old and a civil war veteran, died Saturday, June 14, at his home near Brookneal. Interment was made at Hat Creek on Sunday, the 15th. Mr. Foster was well known in and around Brookneal where he had many friends. He is survived by his wife and six sons, two of whom live in Danville, two reside at home and two, A. A. and Fernal, live in Brookneal; also five daughters, Mrs. W. F. Francis, of Halifax county; Mrs. Percy Davidson, of Rustburg; Mrs. Rufus Epperson and Mrs. Lizzie Epperson, of Campbell county, and Miss Scottie Foster.

Little Billie, the only son of Mr. and Mrs. W. W. Averette, died Wednesday night about 8 o'clock, after and illness of several days. He was 18 months old. The remains will be taken to Farmville for interment.

Acorn-The death angel entered the home of Mr. John Hankley, of Acorn, Sunday afternoon at four o'clock, June 22, and carried away his beloved wife. She was sick only a few days. Her remains were interred in the family burying ground, Monday afternoon in the presence of a large number of loved ones and friends, the service being conducted by her pastor, Rev. J.H. Bass. Mrs. Hankley was a member of Childrey Baptist church from her childhood. She was sincere, modest and active in her Christian life, loyal and devoted to her church. The following were pall bearers; R. L. Roark, W. T. Francis, L. L. Roark, Will Clark, S.H. Roark and Tom Martin. The floral offerings were beautiful and were carried by the following girls; Misses Mamie and Bernice Tribble, Caryn, Thelma and Hildra Woosley, Annie Glass and Mattie Hankley. She is survived by her husband, one daughter, Miss Cora, and three sons, Arthur, Jessie and Johnie, all of whom have our deepest sympathy in their sorrow.

Holly Plain-Mr. Cris Jackson died at his home near Red House Wednesday morning.

July 4, 1919

Elijah M. Jackson (Uncle Chris)-Died at his home near Red House, Charlotte county, Wednesday morning, June 18th, at 3 o'clock, Elijah Maize Jackson. He was born Jan. 5th, 1847. Death was due to paralysis. He had been an invalid for three years. He was an old Confederate veterate (veteran) and was widely known and had many friends. His remains were laid to rest in Trinity cemetery Thursday, June 19, in the presence of a large number of relatives and friends. There were many beautiful floral offerings. He leaves a wife and three children, Mr. W. C. Jackson, of Red House, Mr. C. G. Jackson, of Glen Morgan, W. Va., and one daughter, Mrs. R. W. Rowles, Charlotte CH.

July 11, 1919

The infant daughter of Mr. and Mrs. Leslie Holt died Friday with pneumonia and was buried Saturday at Bethel cemetery.

A few days ago Mr. R. R. Todd received information announcing the death of his brother, Dr. A. S. Todd, of Manning, S.C., who died recently in a Columbia, S.C. hospital where he had been under treatment for the past five weeks.

July 18, 1919

Gladys-July 14-Miss Lizzie Carwile, aged 23 years, died at her home near here last Tuesday at 2:30 o'clock.
Her death was due to consumption and she was a member of Sharon Methodist church at Naruna.
She is survived by her father, Mr. Pierce Carwile, two little sisters, Ethel and Margaret and four brothers, William, Reese and Arthur Carwile of this place and Ruby Carwile, of Lynchburg.
The funeral services were conducted by her pastor, Rev. J. B. Lavinder, at Wesleybury church at Gladys where her body was laid to rest in the presence of a large number of relatives and friends.

Hon. Thos. B. Clark, one of the best known men of Halifax county, died at his home at Clarkton Wednesday of last week at the age of sixty-eight years. Mr. Clark represented his county at one time in the Virginia legislature and was an active citizen until a few years ago when he had to retire on account of ill health. He was prominent in church affairs and one of the largest farmers of the county, having owned a magnificent plantation on Staunton river.

Card of Thanks-Mr. and Mrs. W. W. Averett wish to extend their sincere thanks to the many good people of Brookneal for the kindnesses shown during our recent bereavement in the loss of our little son.

In Memoriam-Whereas, God in His all-wise and unerring providence, has seen fit to call from her earthly labors to her heavenly reward Miss Bernice Suddith, one of our most dearly beloved members, and one deeply interested in missions, we the Womans Missionary Union of Kedron Baptist church adopted the following resolutions:
Resolved, That while we bow with perfect submission to what we recognize as the will of our Heavenly father, we deeply lament her

absence, and we sorrow for the school children most especially since she was a most excellent instructor and loved without an exception by every child.

Resolved, That we will cherish the memory of this devoted christian and strive to emulate her cheery disposition which was a benediction to all with whom she came in contact.

Resolved, That a copy of these resolutions be recorded in our minutes, a copy sent to the bereaved family and a copy sent to the county papers.

Mrs. G. S. Thomas Mrs. L. D. Morgan

August 1, 1919

Slain by Hun Prisoner-Lynchburg information has been received here of the awarding of a posthumous Distinguished Service Medal to Lieutenant J. Beverly Burks, who went to France as a member of Company I, One hundred and sixteenth infantry, Twenty ninth Division from this city.

Lieutenant Burks was killed by a prisoner who was among a number of captured Huns who were being taken back to the rear by a detachment of men under his command. This occurred last October and he was commended for extraordinary heroism on October 23, 1918, the date of his death. His parents, Mr. and Mrs. R. H. Burks, now reside in Newport News, but several other members of his family reside here.

On the afternoon of July 1st, 1919, after an illness of short duration, Mrs. Emma Thornton Coates passed quietly but triumphantly out to her reward. She was born in Halifax county February 29, 1844, the daughter of C.T.C. Carr and Mary Jane Thornton.

She was twice married. Her first husband was Dr. Felix Flournoy Thornton, to whom she was united in marriage December 21, 1869. Although the only child born of this union died at birth, they reared five children, all of whom survive to mourn their loss. The oldest of these is her sister, Mrs. W. M. Bates of Brookneal. The others are: Mrs. W. A. Brumfield, of Richmond; Mrs. E. L. Mealer, Miss Bessie Hobson, of Natalie, and J. Frank Thornton, of Rustburg. She also has one other sister, Mrs. T. H. Claytor, of Bedford, and one brother, Mr. W. C. Carr, of Brookneal.

Dr. Thornton died in February 1899, and on the 2d of November, 1905, she was married to Mr. W. W. Coates, of Natalie, who preceded her to the grave four years ago.

Her entire life was one of devoted service to her family, her friends and her God, and the good she has done will live for generations after her. The lives she has touched must be a sweeter, purer, nobier and gentler for having come in contact with one who, at all times and all places, lived a simple, consistent, christian life. The poor and unfortunate of the community always found in her sympathy and aid, though the world never knew the good she was doing.

Those who had the privilege of looking upon her sweet face cold in death realized that she had been "all the way with Jesus." How sweet is the death of a christian. Death had no sting for her; it was merely an awakening into the eternal, glorious life beyond the skies, where she went to join her loved ones gone before.

The funeral services were conducted by Rev. J. B. Lavinder, after which her body was laid beside her her first husband at the old Thornton home. The throng of friends who gathered there to pay their last tribute or respect to the deceased gave evidence of the love and esteem with which she was held. "To live in the hearts of those we leave behind us is no to die."

A Friend

Charlotte Border-Edward, the infant son of Mr. and Mrs. Jack Bentley, died last Thursday, the 24th, after a long illness. The remains were laid in the White's Chapel cemetery in the presence of a large number of friends. The funeral was conducted Friday afternoon at 5 o'clock by Rev. A. K. Lambkin. The pall bearers were C. H. Marshall, W. T. Cocke, T. T. Mason and Stuart Andrews. The flowers were carried by little Mamie Elliott, Louise Elliott, Elsie Mason and Mrs. C. H. Marshall.

Dies in Western State-Lynchburg-Mrs. Henrietta Bennett Thurman, eighty-one years of age, a native of Bedford county, died at her home in Rolls, Mo. She was a daughter of the Colonel and Mrs. Edward D. Williams and her grandfather, Gray Jones was a Revolutionary soldier. She was the widow of Samuel B. Thurman, who died here many years ago following which she went West with her children. She has but one daughter living now,

Mrs. Annie Schults, of Rolls.

August 8, 1919

Our home was made sad on the 13th of June when the death angel
came and took from us out darling little boy, Jack Randolph, Jr.,
aged two years and nine months, the pride of his home and joy of
our lives. Oh, how we miss him with his affectionate way, with his
hugs and kisses! He would so often come to us, put his precious
little arms about our necks and say, "I love you mother; I love you
daddy."
He was loved by all who knew him. He was so very bright. God
giveth and God taketh away, though it seems so hard to think He
took all we had and left us alone, not even one little sunbeam left
for us. Our dear child was taken from us so unexpectedly. He was
sick only ten days. We loved him well but Jesus loved him best.
We hope to meet him in that bright world above where there is no
pain or sorrow. May God give us strength to bear this trouble.
His Mother

Mrs. Victoria Foster, wife of J. Y. Foster, departed this life July
23d at her home near Brookneal, after a short illness. She is
survived by her husband and the following children: Willie Creed,
Sandy and Scott of Brookneal, Mrs. Rad Foster, all of Lynchburg;
Mrs. Ed Dawson, of Monroe; Mrs Yancy Sublett and Mrs. Henry
Smith, of Brookneal. She was 72 years old and for quite a number
of years a quiet, consistent member of Hat Creek Presbyterian
church, in which cemetery she was laid to rest, the funeral being
conducted by her pastor, Rev. J. A. Scott. The hymns, "How Firm
a Foundation," "Asleep in Jesus," were sung in the church: "My
Jesus I love thee," "Sweet Bye and Bye" and "Shall we gather at
the river" were sung at the grave. Her grandsons, Messrs.
Courtney, Earl, Clayton, Edwin and Hoyt Foster and Andrew
Sublett were pall bearers, and her granddaughters, Misses Annie
and Bessie Foster, Lillie M. Smith, Mrs. Grace Hancock, Mrs. Ola
Sylvy, also Miss Lucy Reynolds, were flowergirls. She leaves a
host of friends and relatives to mourn her departure.

August 15, 1919

Mrs. James Marshall died at her home Sunday from a complication of diseases. Interment was made at the family burying grounds. She leaves a daughter and two sons.

August 22, 1919

Mr. George Mayberry, of Winfall, Va. died Aug. 14, aged 64 years. He leaves to mourn his loss, his wife, Mrs. Flora Mayberry, and six children, Mrs. Sam Daniel, Mrs. Nola Phillips, Mrs. Alice Woodall and Mrs. Gracie Brown Malcolm, of Melrose and Otis and Lawton at home. Funeral services were held at the Diamond Hill church. Interment was in the Diamond Hill cemetery.

Young Man Drowned-Isaac H. Crews, aged 19, was drowned in Barnett's Pond near Roxboro, N.C., last Sunday afternoon while in bathing. He, with four companions, rowed out into deep water in a small boat which was capsized and he being unable to swim, was drowned. Some of his companions nearly lost their lives while trying to save him. The body was recovered and brought back to his home in Halifax county where if was interred at Ellis Creek Baptist church Monday afternoon. Mr. Crews had just finished his course in school and accepted a position with the Boston National Bank. He was very popular and had a large host of friends. He was prominently related in both Halifax and Campbell counties.

Evergreen R.F.D. 1-Dr. Mott Robertson died last night. He had been ill for some time. He will be greatly missed.

Mr. P. M. Hannah died suddenly Wednesday, the 13th, his death being caused from heart trouble. He will be greatly missed in his community.

August 29, 1919

We deeply sympathize with Mr. B. D. Crews and family in the death of his son, Isaac Henry, which occurred in North Carolina on the 17th inst. May God's richest blessings rest and abide in his home.

September 5, 1919

Mrs. C. C. Simpson, of near Altavista, died at Catawba Sanatoruim on Wednesday. The remains were brought home yesterday for interment. Mrs. Simpson was the mother of Mrs. S. T. Jacobs, of Brookneal.

Unveiling of Memorial Tablet-A Memorial Tablet will be unveiled at Hat Creek Presbyterian church on Sunday, Sept. 14th at 4 p.m.-sun time- in memory of Lacy Carey, Henry Lee Foster and Berkeley Bailey, members of this church, who fell in the Meuse-Argonne battle in France.
The address will be made by B. F. Ginther, of Brookneal.
All soldiers who served in the recent war are invited to be present wearing uniforms, and to sit in seats at the front. The public generally is invited to be present.
J. A. Scott, Pastor
NOTE-All soldiers from Halifax county and the vicinity of Brookneal are requested to meet at Brookneal about one hour before the time set for the unveiling and go from here to Hat Creek in automobiles. Arriving at Hat Creek they will join the soldiers from that neighborhood at J. R. Lawson's store and march to the church in company formation. All are requested to wear uniforms but those who for any reason can not appear in uniform should come anyway.

Mrs. Lottie E. Marshall died at her home near Red House, Va. on August 10, after a long illness. For many years her sufferings had been great mentally and physically. She bore her affliction with patience, fortitude and resignation with a christian hope that "Our light affliction which is but for a moment, working for us a far more exceeding and eternal weight of glory." She had been a member of Providence Baptist church for 25 years. She is survived by three children, Macca B., Henry W. and Walter T. Marshall. She was laid to rest in the family burying ground at the home of her grandfather, Dr. Robt. Smith.

September 12, 1919

Sad Death of Little Child-The saddest day that has entered the home of Mr. and Mrs. George Puckett, of Poortown, was last Sunday afternoon when their baby boy, Russell, while out at play with other children fell into a pit and was drowned before anyone could get him out. How sad it is to give the little one up, but God makes no mistakes. To the loved ones we say, weep not, for the little one is safe with Jesus. He is survived by father, mother, two sisters and three brothers. He was very bright and was loved by all who knew him. Written by his cousin, Gracie Guthrie
Editors Note-Owing to lack of time for composition we were compelled to omit several verses of obituary poetry which accompanied the above. The whole section of Campbell and Halifax counties deeply sympathize with Mr. and Mrs. Puckett in their sad bereavement.

Julia Wade, an elderly colored woman, of Rabat, Halifax county, died Wednesday and was buried Thursday, Rev. Ben Hundlay, of Brookneal, conducting the funeral service.

September 19, 1919

Memorial Service at Hat Creek-Tablet Unveiled to Memory of Soldiers who Fell in France
A fine tribute was paid to the memory of three Campbell county boys who fell in France, when on last Sunday afternoon a tablet was unveiled with appropriate ceremonies in the Hat Creek Presbyterian church, of which they were members. The church was filled to full capacity, many standing in the aisles while there were no less than as many more on the outside. The service was under the direction of the pastor, Rev. J. A. Scott, D. D., and the address was made by B. F. Ginther of Brookneal. A very touching part of the ceremony was when the veil, an American flag, was removed by Henry Lee Foster, Jr. the little son of Henry Lee Foster, one of the deceased soldiers. There were fifty-four soldiers present in uniform and several more in citizens' clothes who took part in the service. The soldiers assembled at Lawson's store and marched in a body to the church where they took their places on the front seats, and at the proper time during the ceremony the

soldiers rose in a body and saluted as a tribute to their departed comrades. The choir rendered music appropriate to the occasion and the service throughout was carefully arranged and well carried out. The tablet is of bronze and is fixed in the wall of the church to the right of the pulpit and bears the following inscription:
In Memory of
LACY CAREY
Died Sept. 26, 1918
HENRY LEE FOSTER
Died Sept. 28, 1918
COURTNEY BERKELEY BAILEY
Died Sept 28, 1918
Members of the Hat Creek Presbyterian Church
They fell in the Meuse-Argonne Battle, France, in the heroic advance of the 4th and 80th Divisions A.E.F.
This tablet placed by loving hands shall record their lasting fame.

September 26, 1919

Mr. and Mrs. W. R. Walker were called to Lynchburg Tuesday by the death of Mrs. Walker's sister, Mrs. A. S. Hester, who died suddenly of heart disease at 11:30 o'clock Monday night at her home No. 1 Wall Street, Rivermont into which family moved last Saturday. Mrs. Hester is survived by husband and one son, Maurice Hester, two daughters, Misses Mary and Elizabeth Hester; one brother, John W. Hamlett, and one sister, Mrs. W. R. Walker, of Brookneal.

October 3, 1919

The many friends of Mr. W. R. Bennett were saddened to learn of his sudden death in his office at Glen Wilton, where he was employed as agent for the C & O railway. He was agent here for the Virginian railway for several years.

A number of people from this section attended the funeral and burial of Mr. Charlie Joy at Union Hill on last Tuesday. There was an immense crowd present and a profusion of lovely flowers.

October 10, 1919

Mrs. R. H. McGann died at her home near Hat Creek on Sunday, Sept. 28, at the age of 59 years, after a lingering illness. Mrs. McGann was twice married, first to Mr. Thos. A. Pulliam, and after his death to Mr. R. H. McGann. She is survived by her husband and three brothers, Wince, Jack and John Tibbs.

Given Life Sentence-Lawrence Guthrie, a Halifax county negro who some months ago confessed to killing his wife and then burning her body, has been convicted by a jury in the Halifax county court and sentenced to spend the rest of his life in the penitentiary. The jury's verdict was for first degree murder. A motion for a new trial has been made.

James M. Terry was born at Brookneal, Va. on Dec. 6, 1844 and departed this life Wednesday, Oct. 1st, 1919, at the age of seventy-five. Mr. Terry is survived by four brothers, J. O. Terry, of Brookneal; H. L. Terry, of Washington; I. F. Terry, of Chattanooga, Tenn., and Rev. H. B. Terry, of Jackson, Tenn.; and two sisters, Mmes. W. M. Puckett, of Brookneal and Mollie Maddox, of Chattanooga, Tenn.
At the beginning of the civil war Mr. Terry was living with Jeffress & Jeffress, who kept the only store then in existence in South Boston, the building standing on the site of the present Southern passenger depot. He left the service of his employers to enter the Confederate army and served throughout the war, being at Appomattox at the time of the surrender. After the war he came home and assisted his father and mother in raising and educating his brothers and sisters. He afterwards removed to Terryville where he remained for about ten years, but still looked after his father and mother. Upon the death of his father he came back to the old home and took care of his mother until her death. Soon after her death he had a severe spell of sickness from which he never fully recovered, and was taken by his brother, Mr. J. O. Terry, to his home with whom he remained until his death. The remains were laid to rest at the old family burying ground about two miles east of Brookneal. Thursday afternoon, October 2 with Masonic honors, he having been a member of that fraternity for many years, The funeral services were conducted by Dr. W. F.

Fisher.

October 17, 1919

Killed By Dynamite-A young man named Trent was fatally injured on Thursday of last week near Rustburg while blowing up tree stumps. His parents both died of influenza last fall.

October 24, 1919

Card of Thanks-We wish to thank our friends for the kindness and sympathy shown us in our recent trouble in the death and burial of our darling little babe and also for the beautiful floral offerings. Mr. and Mrs. John E. Hunter Evol. October 20, 1919

William D. Price, aged 75 years, died recently at the home of his daughter, Mrs. C. P. Marshall, near Red House, with whom he had made his home for several years. He had been in feeble health for several years and his death was not unexpected. He was a native of Campbell county.

In Memoriam-In fond remembrance of our faithful and loving husband and father, Mr. William C. Shotwell. He has left us, oh! So sad! Everything seems so gloomy. We can hear his footsteps everywhere we go and we look for him just as we used to; but God has taken our dear father from us to a better world, and we all hope to meet him on that golden shore where sorrow is never known.
By his devoted Wife and Children

Mr. William C. Shotwell died at his home in Brookneal, Thursday evening, Oct. 16, 1919. The funeral was conducted by Rev. W. F. Fisher at Mulberry church in Halifax county Saturday at 3:30. The burial was in Mulberry cemetery. Many beautiful floral offerings were placed upon the grave. Mr. Shotwell is survived by his wife and five children, as follows; Mmes. J. C. Craft and Thomas Golden; J. H. Shotwell, of Norfolk; O. G., of Halifax, and S. F., of Brookneal.

October 31, 1919

The funeral services of the twin boys of Mr. and Mrs. N. R. Patrick were held by Rev. J. W. Bouldin, of the M.F. church. Norman Robert Patrick died on Wednesday, the 22^d, aged 18 days and Henry Thomas Patrick, III, died Thursday, the 23^d, aged 19 days, after a brief illness.

Charlotte County News-Samuel B. Collins, 75 years of age, a prosperous farmer of Charlotte county, died Thursday of last week in Lynchburg, where he had been under treatment about six weeks. His death was due to broncho pneumonia. His body was taken to Drakes Branch for burial.
Mr. Collins was a Confederate veteran having served the last two years in the Confederate Army during the civil war. He is survived by his wife and seven children. They are; T. W. Collins, Keysville, Mrs. J. W. Dickerson, Danville, W. R. Collins, Richmond and V. S., S. H., S. J. and C. B. Collins, Drakes Branch.

Lynchburg-"Aunt" Lettie Elisa Johnson, a colored woman of the old regime, who was known to have been 105 years of age, is dead at the home of C. S. Hutter, in Campbell county. For eighty years she has been a cook in the Hutter family.

Card of Thanks-We wish to thank our many friends for the kindness and sympathy shown to us in our recent trouble, the death of our daughter, (Kathleen) Mrs. S. L. Maddox, also for the beautiful flowers.
Mr. and Mrs. I. H. Vassar Oct 28th, 1919.

In Memoriam-In sad but loving remembrance of our dear little Harry C. Robey, who departed this life three years ago, October 31, 1916.
In our hearts come the bitter cry,
Why oh why did little Harry die?
His vacant chair in our home is stilled
And it can never never be filled.
Following upward we will trod
In the footsteps of our God,
Lord, it is thee that we adore-

For we will meet Harry on that beautiful shore.
By his devoted Mother and Sister

Hat Creek-We were very sorry to hear of the recent death of Mrs. Louis Valley, of Lynchburg. She was a sister of Mrs. Peter Elder, of Crosby. She was laid to rest at Ebenezer cemetery Sunday morning a 9 o'clock. Funeral services were conducted by Rev. A. I. Caudle.

Our hearts go out in sympathy to the many loved ones and friends of Mrs. Sam Maddox, who died Oct. 20th, after an illness of several months. At her request she was buried at the home of her father, Mr. Vasser. The burial services were conducted by her pastor Rev. A. Walter Roten. A large crowd was present and the floral offerings were numerous and beautiful.

November 7, 1919

Halifax County News-Mr. J. J. Hudson died on Oct. 22 at his home near Nathalie, aged about 82 years. He had been affected with heart trouble for some time and had been in declining health for a year or more. He was a Confederate veteran, having served in the cavalry under General Price. He is survived by his wife, three brothers, Elijah Hudson, of Tennessee, T. L. and Elisha Hudson of Halifax county, four sons, R. L., T. J., Chas. and David, three daughters, Mrs. J. S. Newbill, Mrs. Claude Anderson and Mrs. B. L. McCraw and forty-five grandchildren. The remains were laid to rest near his home on a spot which he had selected. Six of his grandsons were the pallbearers; Herbert, Clay, Percy, Clarence and Roy Hudson and Hampton Newhill. The flowers, which were many and beautiful, were borne by his grandchildren. Rev. G. C. Duncan, his pastor conducted the burial service which was attended by a large number if friends.

November 21, 1919

Halifax County News-Mrs. White died several days ago at her home near Fort Mitchell. Her death was due to paralysis. She was advanced in years and is survived by several children and grandchildren.

Charlotte County News-W. R. Morton, an elderly citizen of Charlotte county, died at his home near Keysville, Nov. 8. He is survived by a large family and also leaves a host of friends, being well liked in his home community.

The little son of Mr. and Mrs. Cleveland Carter, who lived near Retirement, was accidentally drowned a few days ago. It is supposed that he was playing near the spring when he fell in face foremost, and was dead when found.

The death of Mrs. Lillie Jordan occurred Saturday. She was a good Christian lady and will be greatly missed. She leaves a husband and three children to mourn their loss.

November 28, 1919

Mrs. A. B. Crawley was called to Lynchburg last week to attend the burial of her brother, Paul W. Landrum. He died quite suddenly, although his health had been frail for a number of years, he having been a great sufferer with asthma. He died on Wednesday, Nov. 19, and was laid to rest beside his father in the Presbyterian cemetery on Friday, Nov. 21. His grave was covered with a profusion of lovely flowers and the large crowd present attested his popularity. He left a wife, one son and three daughters, an aged mother, three sisters and five brothers. Sleep on, dear brother, may we meet in that beautiful city where suffering and parting are no more.

In Memoriam-In sad and loving remembrance of my dear Aunt Lillian Jordan, wife of W. F. Jordan. She died with heart disease in a Lynchburg hospital Nov. 15, 1919 She leaves her husband, three children, father and four brothers, all of Campbell county, to mourn their loss.
Days of sadness still come o'er us,
Tears of sorrow often flow,
Tho' fond memory keeps her with us,
Heaven claimed her one week ago.
Dearest Aunt Lillian, how we miss you,
Miss you more than words can tell,

But we hope some day to meet you,
And together we will dwell.
You are not forgotten, Aunt Lillian,
And never will you be;
For as long as this life claims us,
We will e'er remember thee.
I often sit and think of you, dear,
Now that I am all alone,
For fond memory is the only thing,
That grief can call it's own.
'Tis hard to break the tender cord
With which love has bound our hearts,
"Tis hard, so hard, to speak the words,
We must forever part.
From this world of grief and trouble
To the land of peaceful rest,
God has taken our loved one from us
There to find eternal rest.
Sleep on, our beloved,
Sleep, and take thy rest;
We loved thee, oh, so well, dear,
But Jesus loved thee best.
Written by her loving niece, Annie Guthrie

December 5, 1919

Evol-We have just learned that Mr. Jack Cardwell died at his
home near Early's Chapel on Sunday night. He leaves a large
family and numberless friends who sympathize with the family.

Mrs. A. B. Crawley received information last week of the death of
her nephew, the little 3 year old son of Mrs. Esmond Moore, of
Flatwoods, W. Va. The little one had been an invalid since having
the flu last December, at which time his father died of the same
disease.

A Sad Accident-Probably one of the saddest accidents that it has
ever been the painful duty of the Union Star to Chronicle, occurred
last Friday afternoon when Eugene, the sixteen year old son of Mr.
and Mrs. C. W. Hunter, of near Naruna, was shot and a most

instantly killed by Herman Ginther, ten year old son of the editor of this paper. Herman, in the company with several little friends about his own age, was playing with a 22 caliber target rifle. They were in the driveway of Foster's Warehouse when Eugene Hunter passed them just as Herman holding the gun at a slightly upward angle, pulled the plunger about half way back and accidentally let it slip out of his fingers, exploding the cartridge, the ball striking Hunter just back of and above the right ear. The boys saw him fall and ran to the printing office to tell Mr. Ginther. Young Hunter was carried into the furniture store and everything possible was done for him, but he died in a few minutes without regaining consciousness.

Justice of the Peace J. E. Uzzie, of Naruna was called and empaneled a coroner's jury composed of Messrs. W. W. Averett, Jr., W.R. Walker, N. I. Waltham, T. O. Myers, W. A. Mays and F. H. Henderson. After viewing the remains, visiting the scene of the accident and examining witnesses the jury rendered the following verdict "We the undersigned jury and coroner, find that Eugene Hunter met his death by rifle bullet wound in the head at the hands of Herman Ginther, the discharged of the gun being accidental." The funeral and interment of the victim of the accident took place at Ebenezer church on Saturday afternoon, the services being conducted by Rev. A. I. Caudle. A very large crowd was in attendance, attesting their sympathy for the bereaved family, and the grave was covered with a profusion of beautiful floral designs.

Our community was sadden by the death of Eugene Hunter, who was accidentally shot in Brookneal Friday, Nov. 28th. He leaves to mourn his death father, mother, five sisters and two brothers besides a host of friends. His remains were laid to rest Saturday, Nov. 29th at 3 o'clock at Ebenezer Baptist church, the funeral being conducted by Rev. A. I. Caudle, a host of friends being in attendance.

Our son is gone, he's calmly sleeping,
In death's cold and sad embrace
Lost to us is his dear presence
Vanished is his lovely face.
And the hands that labored for us,
Now are folded on his breast,
While his sweet and gentle spirit,

With the Saviour is at rest.
Oh! dear son, how we miss you
Realizing you are gone,
Tears creep forth from 'neath our lashes
And our hearts are strange alone
While our arms extend in longing
Just to clasp your form once more,
But we know that you are happy,
All in peace on yonder shore.
Farewell, Eugene, not forever
Have you gone from us away
Well we know the separation
Is for only one brief day.
There around God's throne in heaven
Every happiness complete,
We will meet with you, dear Eugene,
And rejoice at Jesus feet.
For Mr. and Mrs. C. W. Hunter and family of Eugene Hunter, the deceased
Written by Annie Sublette, Ruth Sowell, Eura King, Claudia Sublette

Stovall-The death of of Mrs. Harriet Taylor occurred Sunday. She was laid to rest on Monday at the burying ground at Mr. Blackstock's near Stovall.

Spring Mills-Jack Cardwell died at his home near Spring Mills, on Sunday night, Nov. 30th. His remains were interred in the Early Chapel cemetery, Dec. 2nd.

December 12, 1919

Evol-Mrs. Ida Foster and her son-in-law, Newton Joy, of Morris Church, were called by a telegram to Portsmouth last Friday to attend the burial of little Helen Cook, only daughter of Mr. and Mrs. Clayton Cook and grand-daughter of Mrs. Foster. She was accidentally shot and instantly killed by a 16 year old boy. Report says he was entering the house with a loaded gun when the trigger became caught in the portiere and the gun was discharged. The parents have the sympathy of a host of friends.

December 19,1919

Evergreen R.F.D-Mrs. Eugene Threader died recently at a
Lynchburg hospital she had been under treatment.

December 26, 1919

Elijah T. Elder passed quietly away at his home near Brookneal
last Saturday morning after a lingering illness. He is survived by
his wife and five children and other relatives.

Cole's Ferry-Charlie McKinley died at his home near Aspen, Dec.
22^d. He leaves his wife, five children and a large circle of friends
to mourn his death.

January 2, 1920

Stovall-Loyd Waller, son of Mr. and Mrs. Johnnie Waller, died Dec. 24 and was laid to rest at Clover Bottom Baptist church. He was a member of the Baptist Sunday school and will be greatly missed.

Acorn-On the 23^d Earlie Glass died in a South Boston hospital. The remains were laid to rest near Volens on the 25th by the Woodmen of the world, of which order he was a member. He leaves a widow and several small children.

There were two deaths in our community recently. Henry Anderson lost his wife on the 20th and on the 21st the remains were laid to rest in the old family burying ground. Her pastor, Rev. J. H. Bass, conducted the burial services. Many of her friends and relatives came to pay the last tribute of respect.

January 9, 1920

Mrs. Mary Susan Wilson died of paralysis at her home in Charlotte county on Dec. 25, aged 75 years. She leaves her husband, two sons and one brother to mourn her death.

Evol-The friends of Wood Torrence, in this neighborhood, were sorry to learn of his death which occurred at his home near Early's Chapel last week.

Mr. R. O. Elder died at his home near Red Oak on last Thursday and was buried at the family cemetery on the following day.

January 16, 1920

Editor Dies Suddenly-John L. Douglas, Jr., editor of the Altavista Journal, was found dead in his bead (bed) at his father's home at Lynch's on Saturday afternoon at 2 o'clock. He had been complaining of not feeling well for about a week. His body was
118

viewed by Dr. Board, who considered an inquest unnecessary. Heart disease is thought to have been the cause of death. Mr. Douglas was educated at Randolph Macon Academy and Washington and Lee University. He was 34 years of age and unmarried. At the outbreak of the war he enlisted in the Navy on the battleship Charleston and made several trips across to France with the troops. About the first of last May he became editor of the Altavista Journal. He is survived by his father, John L. Douglas, of Lynchs', three brothers, Charles A., and L. E. Douglas, of Lynch's, and Rev. James Douglas, of Atlanta; also, one sister, Miss Margaret Douglas of Lynch's.
The burial took place Monday morning at 11 o'clock at Mt. Hermon church at Lynch's.

Clarkton, R.F.D. 2-The death angel entered the home of Reecy McKinney and took away his beloved wife. She was laid to rest in the family burying ground at the Walker place at 2 o'clock p.m. on January 9th, the funeral service being conducted by Rev. G. W. Ribble.

The death angel entered the home of Mrs. Rosa Bell Crank and took away her eldest daughter, Sallie Bell. She was sixteen years of age and was only sick eleven days. She was a member of the Episcopal church and the funeral service was conducted by Rev. G. W. Ribble. She was laid to rest in the family burying ground at the Adams place on last Friday at 3 o'clock p.m. She left to mourn her loss her mother, two sisters, Gracie May and Adell, and her aged grandmother and several uncles and aunts.

Evol-We were sorry to see in Sunday's News that Mr. John L. Douglas editor of the Altavista Journal, died quite suddenly on last Saturday. The family has our sympathy.

Mrs. Robert Tibbs died quite suddenly last week at her home near Union Hill. She had been in frail health quite a while. She was a consistent member of Union Hill church and will be greatly missed. The family have the sympathy of a large circle of friends.

Aspen-We were very sorry to hear of the death of Mrs. R. Kittredge, who formerly lived near here, but recently left for Ohio.

January 23, 1920

The people of this community were very sorry to hear of the death of John L. Douglas, Jr., at Lynch's Sation last Saturday.

The death angel entered the home of Mr. and Mrs. Elmo Waller on the 18th and took away their baby. It was laid to rest in the family burying ground on the 19th.

Plum Branch-Miss Vivian Torrence, who has been staying with her mother since her father's death, returned to Lynchburg last Sunday.

February 6, 1920

Evol-The death of Mr. Tom Franklin occurred in Detroit on Saturday morning. He was one of our Campbell boys and was a victim of the influenza. He leaves six brothers and three sisters. Our sympathy goes out to them.

Fork of Falling-Mrs. Maggie Fortune and Miss Gracie Carey were called from Lynchburg by the death of their grandmother, Mrs. M. J. Harper.

The community was saddened by the death of one of our oldest ladies, Mrs. Mary Jane Harper, who died on the 28th. She would have been 85 years old the 5th of Feb., had she lived until then.

Harrisburg-Uncle Wyat Harvey, colored, died January 25.

February 13, 1920

Mrs. W. A. Bass received a message a few days ago announcing the death of her brother, Gette Davenport, at Rodden.

Information was received here Thursday morning to the effect that R. Lit Mays, a former resident of Brookneal, died Wednesday night at his home in Lynchburg, of pneumonia following an attack of influenza.

Gladys-Our community was made sad last week by the death of Mrs. Massie Phillips, who at the time of her death was living in Roanoke, but up to less than two months ago was a resident of near here. Influenza followed by pneumonia was the cause of her death. Her remains were brought here and laid to rest in the cemetery at Wesleybury, where she was a member. Funeral services were conducted by her pastor, Rev. E. R. Crawley and the Baptist minister, Rev. A. M. Padgett. She leaves her husband and son, and several brothers and sisters.

The Hero of Red Hill-There died at Red Hill a few years ago Dr. Thomas Stanhope Henry. Pereaps (perhaps)no member of the Henry family did as much for others as did he.
Maybe it was forty years ago when lagrippe struck this country. People were coming down with it in every family and he was kept so busy (he being the only doctor) that he had no rest, night or day. I had always helped the sick around me and when the negroes in the cabins on our place and in those on Mr. Maloney's sent begging me to come and see if I could help them, as they were having "such high fevers," I swallowed an assafoetida pill and went on. I had met Dr. Henry and he asked me to help him, for he had nobody else. The only person in his house his cook, had been hauled home in a wagon sick. He said those who placed around their necks a string with a bag containing gum camphor, powered snake-root and a little assafoetida and wore it till the disease wore itself out of the air-provided they had not been exposed themselves before using the prevention-would not have it; and they did not. Dr. Frank Deane, of Richmond, kept the smallpox from his clientele with the same remedy. He had expressed a fear that he had applied the prevention two late in his own case, and said this "grippe"- the same thing as flu-is the old disease once called "the relapsing disease" because if the patient exerted himself too soon he would suffer more in the relapse than in the original state.
He gave me (his "assistant") lots of powered seneca snake-root, some camphor, assafoetida and a little ipecac, with instructions to make all the people wear the bags for prevention, and to brew a strong snake-root tea for every patient whom I could walk to see, and drop in a pitcher a little ipecac and pour the tea on it and stir it, forcing them to drink it freely-use it for water.

He gave me a vial of croton oil to rub on the chests to save the lungs, and as the disease made them very weak, to diet them on nothing but milk, toddy or eggnog. He had me visit all the patients in walking distance and had more than he could do on his horse, but we lost no patients that we got to before they were about to die anyway, and the hero, going day and night, wore himself out and one morning I went to report to him and found him down with it. He was so glad to see me come in he cried for joy. I made him as easy as I could and came for my husband who went to the stable and attended the doctor's horse, to the relief of him and the horse. We nursed him back to health by his own directions. He said he had lost one lung at sixteen and must care for the other to the end. (84 years was the end) and knowing that everything depended on the one lung he was compelled to make a special lung study, and had satisfied himself that the snake-root tea with a little ipecac had cured numerous cases of pneumonia with all its complications. He ordered me home to rest and made my husband wait on him, but I sent him jellies, etc., and the whole neighborhood rejoiced to see our hero well again.

Dr. Henry was the last grandson of Patrick Henry to die.

"An Ounce of Precaution."

E. I. Baldwin

Oakdale (Campbell County)-Mrs. Tommie Pentecost died Feb. 6th at her home at Spring Mills.

Evergreen, R.F.D.-Mrs. Laura Marshall died in Staunton on February 2d. Her remains were laid to rest in the family burying ground here.

Walter Childress died in West Virginia recently. His remains were brought to his old home place and laid to rest in the family burying ground. He is survived by his mother and three sisters.

February 20, 1920

Card of Thanks-We wish to thank the many friends and neighbors for the sympathy and kindness which was shown us during the sickness of Mr. Nash and death of our darling baby. May God bless them.

Mr. and Mrs. S. H. Nash, Phenix, Va.

Miss Labinda Lipscomb died at the home of her niece, Mrs. A. T. Thornton, last Friday morning at 10:30 o'clock after a brief illness from pneumonia. Interment took place in the Wickliffe cemetery, adjoining the Presbyterian church, Saturday afternoon at 3 o'clock, the funeral service being conducted by Dr. W. F. Fisher, pastor of the Baptist church, assisted by Rev.'s J. B Lavinder and John B. Williams. The pallbearers were W. R. Walker, R. F. Connally, T. O. Myers, T. O. Bates, J. H. Booker and W. A. Mays.

Miss Lipscomb was preceeded to the grave several years ago by her parents. She is survived by two brothers, Robert Lipscomb, of Rock Hill, S.C., and R. T. Lipscomb, of Malden Mass., and one sister, Mrs. Fannie E. Williamson, of Charlotte, N.C. She was 66 years of age.

Miss Lipscomb had made her home with her niece, Mrs. A. T. Thornton, for the past twelve years, during which period she became devoted to Mrs. Thornton's children, her greatest pleasure in life being found in service to these children whose love for her was attested by the beautiful floral design they had placed on the grave.

On Feb. 12, 1920, the death angel entered the home of Mr. W. H. Coates and bore away the spirit of his beloved wife. Her death was caused by cancer, from which she had been a sufferer for about four years. Mrs. Coates was operated on several times but she was never relieved of her suffering. She bore her affliction with fortitude and was always cheerful. She was, before her her marriage, Miss Eula Carr, of Halifax county. She was a devoted wife and mother and an earnest christian, having been a member of Kedron Baptist church since she had been in this county. She was 49 years old and survived by her husband and four children as follows: Mrs. Frank Thornton, of Lynchburg; Mrs. Felix Claytor, of New Chapel; Messrs. W. C. and W. P. Coates, of Gladys. She was dearly beloved by all who knew her and she will be greatly missed in her home and community. Interment took place in the family burying grounds in Halifax county. The sympathy of the entire community is extended to the bereaved family.

Stovall-We were all sorry to learn of the death of Miss Cornelia Francis, who died Feb. 8th. She was laid to rest in the family burying ground near Stovall.

Mike-Mrs. Sallie Cawthorne and Mr. and Mrs. Moody Martin were notified last week of the death of Meriam, the little daughter of Mr. and Mrs. Rosser Wolridge. Our deepest sympathy is extended to them in their bereavement.

Morris Church-On the 7th inst. Mrs. O. L. Pentecost passed away, her death being caused by consumption. Interment was in the family burying ground near Morris Church.

Cody-Elmo Waller's children are still sick from the effects of whooping cough. Mr. Waller lost an infant daughter with whooping cough recently.

S. W. East was called recently to the bedside of his dying uncle, J. R. Maddox, near Altavista. Mr. Maddox lived only four hours after Mr. East reached his bedside. He leaves a wife 78 years old, who has been bedridden for more than two years. He died on the 13th and was buried on the 14th in the family burying ground.

Rustburg-Miss Nora Crickenburger, principal of the high school, was called to her home on account of the death of her sister-in-law.

Mrs. J. W. Bouldin was called to Danville by a telegram announcing the death of her father, Mr. Howard.

February 27, 1920

Mrs. Amanda Jane Adams, wife of the late R. E. Adams, of Halifax county, died Sunday morning at eight o'clock at the home of her stepson, Mr. Jesse T. Adams, about six miles from Brookneal, in Halifax county.
Mrs. Adams was 83 years old last November, and is survived by two brothers, T. W. Gilliam, of Lynchburg and W. F. Gilliam, of Naruna.
The interment took place Monday afternoon at 2:30 o'clock at the old home place, near Naruna, being conducted by Rev. John B. Williams.

Mrs. A. B. Crawley received a message last week notifying of the death of her niece, Mrs. Edwin Morrison, at Summersville, Oregon. She had pneumonia following the flu and all six children are down with the flu now. Mrs. Morrison was a daughter of E. Gibbs Moore, of Flatwoods, W.Va.- formerly of Concord, Va. – whose letter of appreciation of the Star was published last week.

John William Hubbard died on Feb. 19th, at the home of his father, Samuel C. Hubbard, in Halifax county. He was 29 years of age and his death was caused by pneumonia following an attack of influenza. The remains were laid to rest in the family burying grounds, the funeral service being conducted by Rev. J. B. Lavinder, of Brookneal. The pallbearers were Tom Rudder, Ragsdale Davis, Clinton Francis, Stephen Hubbard, J. Cicero LaPrade and Tommy Guthrie. The floral offerings were borne to the grave by Misses Cary Sales, Flossie Rudder, Caroline Francis, and Mmes. A. T. Thornton, J. C. LaPrade and Richard Tucker. "Billy" as he was affectionately known was a great favorite in the neighborhood. He was noted for his high sense of honor and strength of character and was always ready to be of service to his neighbors in sickness or in any other way, and will be greatly missed.
Besides his aged father he is survived by five brothers and two sisters, as follows: Carrington, Sam, Clem, Robert and Randolph, Janie and Anna. His mother preceded him to the grave just one year ago.

March 5, 1920

Card of Thanks-We wish to thank our friends for their kindness during the sickness and death of Mrs. Amanda J. Adams.
Mr. and Mrs. Jesse T. Adams and family

Miss Nellie Puryear died at her home near here last Thursday and was buried at the cemetery at Wesleybury Friday. The services were conducted by Rev. A. M. Padgett.

Oakdale (Charlotte County)-This neighborhood was very much saddened to learn of the death of little Garnet Dews, who died Feb.

19th with whooping cough, influenza and pneumonia. The many friends extend their heartfelt sympathy to the bereaved family.

March 12, 1920

Gravel Hill (Charlotte County)-We wish to extend our sympathy to Mrs. Tony Lipscomb whose mother died recently.

Card of Thanks-We take this method to thank our many friends and neighbors for the kindness and help during the recent sickness and death of our aunt Miss Emma Puryear.
R. T. Puryear and G. L. Puryear and family

Mr. and Mrs. Obie Compton lost their infant last Saturday. It was buried Sunday in the old burying ground at the G. C. East place.

Naruna-Hubbard Monroe, the little son of Mr. and Mrs. Robert Hurt, died Tuesday, March 2, of influenza. He was three years of age and had always been delicate. Interment was made in the family burying ground Wednesday, March 3rd.

Edge-Mr. and Mrs. Clem Trent lost their little son, only a few hours old, some days ago.

Sam Conthran, son of Hugh Cothran, died at his wife's home near Melrose, on the 19th of February of flu, being ill only a few days. He leaves to mourn his death his wife, two sons and one daughter, his father, one sister and four brothers. He was thirty-three years old.

Marshall Pugh, one of the old soldiers, died at his home Saturday, March 6th. He was buried at Franklin M.E. church Sunday afternoon. He was 94 years old and leaves an aged widow and several sons and daughters.

March 19, 1920

Paul, the 16-year-old son of Mr. and Mrs. Gus Viar, died of pneumonia at their home in Lynchburg Sunday evening. The remains were brought to Naruna for interment Tuesday.

The friends of Mr. and Mrs. Booker Fitch, formerly of Diamond Hill, now of Lynchburg, sympathize with them in the death of their little daughter from pneumonia. She was buried at Diamond Hill Monday.

Card of Thanks-R. F. Francis and family wish to extend their sincere thanks to the many neighbors and friends who showed so much kind consideration and helpfulness during the illness, death and burial of C. C. Adams. Especially do we wish to thank those who contributed so many beautiful flowers.

Riverside Farm-Jim Reynolds of Union Hill neighborhood, was called to Lynchburg recently to attend the funeral and burial of his daughter, Mrs. Nat Madddox.

Craptown-The death angel entered the home of Mr. and Mrs. Emmett Johnson Saturday and took away their little two-year-old daughter, Agnes. She was a victim of whooping cough and pneumonia. The remains were laid to rest Sunday afternoon. The bereaved family have the sympathy of a host of friends.

Red Farm-We were sorry to hear of the death of little Alma Fitch, the youngest daughter of S. B. Fitch, of Lynchburg, formerly of this section. She died of pneumonia following an attack of influenza. She leaves to mourn her loss father, mother, one brother and one sister. She was buried at Diamond Hill Church Monday evening.

Fork of Falling-Mrs. Henry Harper died in a hospital in Lynchburg last Friday and was buried at Beulah Baptist church Saturday afternoon. She leaves her husband and eight little children besides a host of friends to mourn her death.

March 26, 1920

Gladys-Mrs. Hudson Scott, of near this place, died last Sunday after a short illness of flu-pneumonia. Her remains were laid to rest at the cemetery at Wesleyburg. Funeral services were conducted by Rev. F. R. Crawley , assisted by Rev. A. M. Padgett.

Winfall-John Neil and family have been very ill with flu. Four of Mr. Neil's little children died last week of whooping cough, flu and pneumonia. Their bodies were taken to Pittsylvania county for burial.

J. A. Moon was called to Pittsylvania county one day last week on account of the extreme illness of his mother. She died March 17th and was laid to rest in the family burying ground Thursday afternoon at 2 o'clock.

Abell-On the 12th of March, the death angel visited the home of Henry Harper and took away his wife, nee Carrie Holmes Elder, aged 33 years. She is survived by her husband and eight children. She had been in bad health for two months and was taken to Lynchburg hospital one week before her death. Interment was made at Beulah Baptist church Saturday afternoon. Rev. J. D. Kesler officiating. Her brothers acted as pall bearers and Mr. Harper's nieces carried the flowers.

Lynchburg, Va., March 20 (Special)-The death angel entered the home of Mr. and Mrs. S. B. Fitch Sunday, March 14, at 3 o'clock p.m., and claimed for its victim Alma, the youngest daughter. She had not been sick very long and her death came as surprise to her friends.
Alma was nine years old and her death was due to pneumonia following an attack of influenza.
She was laid to rest at Diamond Hill Monday, the 15th, at 2 o'clock p.m. in the presence of a large assembly of sorrowing friends, Rev. A. M. Padgett officiating in a most impressive manner. The hymns sung were "Sometime we will understand," and "God be with you." She is survived by her father and mother, one sister, Armor Fitch and one brother, Raymon Fitch, all of Lynchburg.

April 2, 1920

In Memoriam-In sad but loving remembrance of my lillile (little) boy, Loyd Waller, who entered into life immortal just three months ago today, March 23, 1920.
It's hard, so hard to give him up,

And say that he is gone;
But he is happy with the blest,
While I am left alone.
Often I have looked for him
And oft have seen him come,
But now he has gone from me,
Never to return.
Others there are to comfort me,
But what is life without him?
Where, O, where can comfort be?
'Tis but a vale of sadness.
But when my life's work is ended,
And I join that happy band;
Loyd will tell me why he left me,
Then, oh, then, I'll understand.
We can not, Lord, Thy purpose see,
But though it is hard, I'll not complain,
For all is well that's done by Thee,
And trusting Thee, we'll meet again.
Written by his sad mother.

Naruna-R. R. Bradshaw died several days ago at his home near here with pneumonia, following influenza. The remains were taken to Henry county for burial. He leaves a widow and three children.

A report has reached here that the mail carrier in the Hell Bend section noticed that the mail had not been removed from one of the boxes on his route for several days. He is said to have driven by the house to ascertain the cause of the family's failure to get their mail, and found the mother, father and one child dead in bed from influenza, and a little girl, the only other living human being on the place, very ill with the same disease. The report states the little girl said she had slept on the doorstep two nights, not being able to stay in the house on account of the odor from the bodies of the dead. She had had nothing to eat for several days and was in a pitiable condition. This report may or may not be true. It sounds improbable, yet it is within the realm of possibility, for similar instances have occurred in the influenza epidemic both this year and last. To say the least it points a moral which may well be heeded in the future. Great drives are made for money for relief of distress in foreign countries, while we forget the misery that lies at our own doors and are all too careless of our neighbors welfare, especially during an epidemic of disease. We have peace officers for the enforcement of law and order; why not have health officers whose business it should be to keep a close check on every family, especially those living in isolated places so as to avoid just such occurrences as this rumor relates?

Aunt Sue Ewel, an aged colored woman, died Saturday morning and was buried at St. Luke Sunday afternoon. She was highly respected by both white and colored.

Mrs. W. G. Clay received a telegram Wednesday announcing that some unknown person had called her uncle, Josiah Merryman, who lived in Baltimore, to his door and shot him through his stomach. He was taken to a hospital and died soon after.

W. D. Ferguson, ninety-one years old, a prominent citizen of Appomattox county and a civil war veteran, died at the home of his daughter, Mrs. W. J. Fleshman, at Rolling Hill, Wednesday, March 24, after being confined to his bed for several months. Rev. G. A. Chocklett conducted the funeral service and interment was in the family burying ground at his home. The pall bearers were his grandsons, Floyd and John Ferguson, of Lynchburg; Willie Ferguson, of Evergreen; Wallace Woodson, of Appomattox county; Tom Williamson, of Lynchburg, and Henry Williamson, of Morris Church.
He is survived by the following children: Mrs. W.J. Fleshman, of Rolling Hill; Mrs. J. H. Williamson, of Morris Church; Mrs. Lucian Woodson, of Appomattox county, J. F. Ferguson of Chap, and W. H. Ferguson of Appomattox county. He is also survived by forty grandchildren, forty great-grandchildren and one great-great-grandchild.

Oakdale (Charlotte County)-This neighborhood was very much saddened to hear of the death of Davis Jordan, who died March 24th, in a Richmond hospital. The many friends extend their heartfelt sympathy to the bereaved family.

The death angel visited the home of W. T. Loyd March 18th and took away his beloved wife. She leaves a husband and six small children, six sisters and one brother. Death was due to flu and pneumonia.

Gladys-We deeply sympathize with Mr. Hutson Scott and his children in the death of their wife and mother.

April 9, 1920

Davis B. Jordan died at St. Luke's Hospital, Richmond, Va, March 24, 1920 after an illness of about three weeks. He was a great sufferer but bore his suffering very patiently. Mr. Jordan was a kind and loving husband and father and was liked by all who knew him. He will be greatly missed by his friends and loved ones. All was done for him that could be done by kind and loving hands but God in His wisdom saw best to take him home.
He leaves a wife and seven children, five sons and two daughters. His remains were laid to rest at Midway Baptist Church, the funeral service being conducted by Rev. J. D. Kesler.

Mrs. J. Rice who recently moved to Gladys, died here in her 78th year. The body was taken for burial to Stovall, Halifax county.

In Memoriam-Written in memory of our dear father, C. O. Scott, who died March 29, 1919.
The silver cord was broken,
Brightness left the day,
The spring turned back to winter
When father went away.
We loved him, yes, we loved him,
"But Jesus loved him best;"
He hath heard at last the great Amen,
Hath obtained his soul's request.
There is a song that remaineth
Forever in our ears-
"I need Thee, oh, I need Thee,"
And it always brings the tears
It recalls my fathers visions,
His dreams of days to be,

131

For he ever sang,"I need Thee,
I need Thee, oh, I need Thee."
Shall we listen to father's voice,
Clasp his hand or kiss his brow?
Will the circle be unbroken
When we gather over there?
God in his wisdom only knows,
But this sufficeth,"We shall meet."
His loving daughter

Forest View (Spout Spring,R.F.D.)
Mrs. Daniel Mann died last Friday and was buried Saturday
afternoon at Central church. We extend to this family our
sympathy.

April 9, 1920

Gladys-Mrs. J. Rice who recently moved to Gladys, died here in
her 78th year. The body was taken for burial to Stovall, Halifax
county.

Harvey Pugh, son of Mr. and Mrs. Nathan Pugh, died at his home
near Gladys, from the effects of influenza, age 11. He was buried
at Kedron Baptist church cemetery, the services being conducted
by Rev. A. M. Padgette, assisted by Rev. A. R. Crawley.

Mrs. Daniel Mann died last Friday and was buried Saturday
afternoon at Central church. We extend to this family our
sympathy.

April 23, 1920

Information has been received here of the sudden death of L. O.
Holloway in a hospital at Charlestown, S.C. Mr. Holloway will be
remembered as the senior partner of Holloway, Bowen & Cothran,
proprietors of the Bright Bell Warehouse here.

In Memoriam-There are those who simply pass through life like
"Ships that pass in the night," while others radiate so much love
and kindness that their going away that leaves a real void. Such an

one was Mrs. Elizabeth Langhorne Baldwin, wife of Samuel Baldwin, who entered into the joy of her Lord at the home near Aspen, Va. on Sunday April 11, in the 73rd year of her life.

Oh mother-heart so tender,
So like to that above,
Oh life so free to render,
The lowly deeds of love!
Do we wonder that God called thee?
The wonder is the more
That seeing all thy beauty
He called thee not before.
Kate M. Hunt R.2, Brookneal, Va. April 16, 1920

Evol-Mr. and Mrs. Willie Tanner lost one of their twin babies last week. The little one had always been frail. They have the sympathy of their many friends.

April 30, 1920

The following item concerning the death of L. O. Holloway, well known in Brookneal, is taken from the Charleston, (S.C.) News and Courier.

Lake City-April 19-Special: L.O. Holloway, a widely known man, of Lake City, died Sunday night at 11 o'clock in Charleston in the Baker Sanatorium. He was fifty years of age and was one of the most respected citizens of Lake City, being engaged mostly in the tobacco business.

He came here about fifteen years ago, from Durham, N.C. being sent here by the American Tobacco Company as buyer for them. He held this position until about four years ago, when he joined with G. R. Bowen in buying the brick warehouse owned by J. D. King and in this enterprise he was successful. He married Miss Eva Hollins, who with five children survive him.

Mr. Holloway was taken to Charleston Sunday afternoon by special train over the Atlantic Coast Line and was carried at once to the sanatorium. He was known to be in a desperate condition and it was hoped that an immediate operation would save his life. The J. M. Connelley Company shipped his body to Lake City yesterday afternoon.

May 7, 1920

Tom Webb returned to his home in Richmond Wednesday after being with his mother here in her last illness and death which occurred Sunday night.

Mrs. Grace J. Webb died at her home in Brookneal last Sunday night, aged 74. Her husband Mr. J. M. Webb preceded her to the grave just two years ago. Interment was made in the cemetery here in the presence of a large outpouring of friends of the family, Rev's W. F. Fisher and J. B. Lavender conducting the funeral service. Mrs. Webb is survived by two daughters Misses Effie and Ella, also two sons, J. E., of Brookneal and G. T., of Richmond. She had been a member of the Presbyterian church at Rough Creek since early childhood, and bore her long illness with fortitude. The floral offerings were many and beautiful.

Death of Capt. W. A. Bass-W. A. Bass died suddenly at his home in Brookneal last Saturday night. He was 79 years of age and a veteran of the civil war, having served four years in the Confederate Army. The remains were taken to his old home in Halifax county, Monday for burial. He had been a life-long member of the Baptist church, and a member of the Masonic fraternity for fifty years. He is survived by his wife, four daughters, Mmes. J. J. Blanks, of Houston, G. J. Adams, of Vernon Hill, H. T. Crews and R. A. Johnson, of South Boston, and five sons, G. W. Bass, of Southern Pines, N.C., J. T., of Brookneal, Geo. W., of Danville, W. E. of Lexington, Ky., and Rev. A. B. of Newark, N. J. The Masons of Rodden and Staunton River lodges participated in the funeral ceremony, Rev's. Duncan and Cawley, of the Baptist church, also taking part. The very large gathering at the funeral attested the popularity of the deceased and the esteem in which he was held.

May 14, 1920

Mrs. Willie DeJarnette, wife of Dock DeJarnette, died at her home in Halifax county Sunday afternoon about 3 o'clock. She had been in poor health for some time and her death was not unexpected. She is survived by her husband and four small children, all girls.

She is also survived by her father and mother, Mr. and Mrs. J. A. Guthrie, and three sisters, Mmes. George Puckett, John Davis and Louis Rudder, and five brothers, Ed, Henry, Jesse, O. J., and S. A. Guthrie. Interment was made in the old home burying ground at Mr. James DeJarnette's at 3 o'clock Monday, Rev. W. F. Fisher, of Brookneal, conducting the funeral service. The family have the sympathy of a host of friends.

Little Child Killed by Train-A very sad accident occurred in Brookneal, Monday morning at about 9:30 o'clock, when Marion, the little two year old daughter of Mr. and Mrs. Frank Henderson, was run over and killed by the south-bound local freight train. The child had been playing on the front porch of her home near the scene of the accident, and the mother, not noticing the child leave the porch, was busy with her housework. The child wandered to the track and sat down. When the freight rounded the curve, the engineer and fireman both noticed what they thought was a piece of paper on the track ahead of them, but as the engine rolled forward they realized it was a child. The emergency brake was applied and the engine reversed, but although the train was already being slowed down for its usual Brookneal stop, it was too late and more than half of the train passed over the child's body before it was brought to a standstill. The little body was picked up by Capt. Sowers and laid in the cab and brough to the station. In the meantime Mrs. Henderson, who had missed her little daughter was out searching for her and did not know of the accident until told by neighbors.

The little body was taken to the furniture store of Jere White & Co. where it was prepared for burial. The remains were taken to Lynchburg Monday night and interred Tuesday, a number of friends and relatives of the family accompanying them. The bereaved parents have the heartfelt sympathy of the entire community.

The coroner's jury exonorated the train crew from any blame in the matter, it appearing that the accident was unavoidable.

May 21, 1920

Evol-We have just learned that R. H. Jones who has been ill with Brights Disease quite a while, died at his home near Gladys last night.

May 28, 1920

Perth-We were sorry to hear of the death of Miss Mary Francis, who died Friday morning and was buried Saturday afternoon.

Aspen-The death angel came and took away the darling baby of Mrs. Dug Puckette Friday, aged four months.

Stovall-We are sorry to report the death angel took away our friend, Mr. Buck Landrum, Friday night May 21st. His family has our sympathy.

Wren-Mrs. John Ramsey died at the home of her daughter, Mrs. F. A. Mason, Saturday morning.

Bristol- Mrs. Allen M. Stout, of Mountain City, Tenn., was instantly killed and her husband, a prominent farmer of that place, was seriously injured Sunday when their automobile turned turtle at Damascus, according to advices received here. Faulty steering apparatus was reported to have been the cause of the accident.

Manassas-Karl J. Austin, a crippled insurance agent, who had been held in the county jail here since May 3, charged with murdering R. Bailey Davis, manager of the Davis Brothers' Ice and Fuel Company, was released on $10,000 bond. Austin admits he shot and killed Davis while engaged in a quarrel. He alleges Davis, who was a married man, alienated the affections of Mrs. Austin, who was employed in Washington at the time of the tragedy.

June 4, 1920

Evol-Will Coleman and daughter, Edna, of Kew, attended the burial of the former's father, near Farmville., last Friday. He dropped dead of heart trouble while he was at work in the field. They returned home Friday evening and during that night Miss Edna was taken quite ill, but her condition is now somewhat improved.

June 11, 1920

The little son of Napoleon Walthall, who lives near Naruna, died last Friday after a lingering illness, and was buried Saturday.

Bear Creek-We extend our deepest sympathy to Mr. Oscar Cyrus and daughter in the loss by death wife and mother.

Evol-The friends of Mr. and Mrs. Gilliam Trent will sympathize with them in the death of their daughter, Mrs. Ady Cyrus, who died at a Lynchburg hospital last Thursday.

Mrs. Whit Foster was called on Monday to the bedside of her mother, Mrs. Carwile, near Naruna. The latter is quite ill; she ninety years old and her recovery is doubtful.

Mrs. A. B. Crawley received a telegram last week informing her of the sudden death of her brother-in-law-, E. Gibbs Monroe, of Flatwoods, W. Va. Mr. Moore was a native of Campbell county and resided here all his life till about seventeen years ago.

June 18, 1920

Card of Thanks-We wish to thank our friends and neighbors for many kind deeds shown us during the three months sickness and death of our dear 10 year old son, Louis.
By his mother and father. Nap. and Annie Walthall.

Evergreen, R.F.D.-Mrs. Sidney Hamlet, of near Red House died in a Lynchburg hospital yesterday. Her funeral will be conducted by her pastor, Rev. A. J. Ponton, in Providence Baptist church at Red House, at 3 o'clock this afternoon and her remains will be laid to rest in the family burying ground at their old home place, known as Holly Plain. She is survived by her husband and three children. They have our deepest sympathy.

June 25, 1920

After a prolonged illness, Mrs. Mary Wilburn, the young wife of Mr. C. S. Wilburn, of Long Island, died at the home of her sister,

Mrs. L. V. Bailey, in Brookneal Thursday of last week. Mrs. Williams was a daughter of Mr. and Mrs. R. H. Henderson, of Brookneal, and was very popular. Interment was made at Falling church on Friday afternoon, in the presence of a large concourse of sorrowing friends. Rev. W.F. Fisher conducted the funeral services.

Three Forks-Mr. and Mrs. Holt Dawson went to Danville Monday to attend the burial of Mrs. Dawson's mother, Mrs. C. B. Strictland.

W. T. Tribble, a well known farmer, died at his home in Halifax county, a few miles from Brookneal, Wednesday afternoon at about 4 o'clock. Mr. Tribble, it will be remembered, was shot in the forehead during a raid by revenue officers on an illicit distillery in his neighborhood. Part of his skull was torn away exposing the brain. Mr. Tribble had been undergoing surgical and medical treatment at a Lynchburg hospital since the time of his injury and was thought to be getting along fine, paying frequent visits to his home. It was during one of these visits that meningitis developed and he sank rapidly until the end. Mr. Tribble was a popular and respected citizen and is survived by a large family. Interment was made in the home burying ground Thursday afternoon.

Bear Creek-The infant son of Mr. and Mrs. Charles Williams died Friday afternoon and was buried Saturday. The family have the sympathy of a host of friends.

Miss Ruby Williams, who has a position in Lynchburg, was called home last week by the illness and death of her little brother.

July 2, 1920

Halifax County News-Mr. A. A. Allen, a well known farmer in the Perth neighborhood, died in a Lynchburg hospital last Thursday and was buried Friday near his home. Mr. Allen was about fifty years of age. He is survived by his wife. There was a large outpouring of his friends at the funeral, which was under the auspices of the Masons and Odd Fellows, he being a member of both orders.

Red Oak-Joe James died Wednesday at 9 o'clock and was buried on Friday at his home place. The pall bearers were W. R. Berkley, H. C. Whitlow, W. H. Terry, Aubrey Jones, I. P. Whitlow and Simmie Duffer. He leaves a wife and seven children to mourn his loss.

Melrose-The death angel came Friday in the home of Mr. Jim Robert Davis and took away his kind and loving wife. She left to mourn her death a husband, nine children, aged mother, two sisters and several brothers.

July 9, 1920

Green Hill Road-Mr. and Mrs. G. W. East was called to Pittsylvania county last Friday to attend the funeral of their uncle, John W. East, formerly of that county, but had for the past 19 years resided in Latham, Ohio. He reached home the 28th day of June and lived only three days after his arrival. Heart trouble was the cause of death.

Spring Mills-Mr. Ben Harvey died at his home here on Thursday, June 24th. His death, while not unexpected came as a great shock and cast gloom of sorrow over his host of friends and relatives. The funeral was conducted at Earley's Chapel by his pastor, Rev. Mr. Marsh. He is survived by his wife, who was Miss Fannie Cardewell before her marriage, and one little adopted son, Willie. We wish to extend to them our deepest sympathy.

July 23, 1920

Mr. J. E. McCullough, of Halifax county, died in a Lynchburg hospital Wednesday morning about six o'clock and was taken to his home in Halifax for burial Thursday. Mr. McCullough was nearly 58 years of age. He is survived by his wife, five children and two brothers.

After an illness of more that a year, in which time she was under treatment of the most skilled physicians and surgeons of America, Mrs. Elizabeth Lyons Swanson, wife of United States Senator Claude A. Swanson, died at her home in Washington. Illness was due to a complication of ailments, which baffled medical science. The body was brought here and the funeral took place from St. Paul's Episcopal Church.

Mrs. Swanson was the daughter of the late Dr. Peter and Addie Deans Lyons, and was a native of this city, where she was educated. It was while her husband was governor of Virginia that Mrs. Swanson achieved many social triumphs and successes due to her rare good judgement and splendid tact, discharging her duties as hostess for the Old Dominion at the Jamestown exposition with a skill that won admiration on every side. She had a prominent place in the social life of Washington.

July 30, 1920

Mr. Geo. W. Jones died Saturday afternoon in a Lynchburg hospital where he was operated on last Monday. He was an old confederate soldier, having served in the civil war. He was twice married, first to Miss Gilliam, and then to Miss Elliott. The following children survived him: Mrs. Hugh D. Via, of Roanoke, Mrs. N. A. Tanner, of Winfall; Mrs. T. M. Fitch, of Gladys; Measrs. Marshall Jones, of Washington; W. W. Jones and R. G. Jones, of Gladys; and E. A. Jones, of Winfall, also he has twenty six grandchildren. He has two sisters, Mrs. Emmett Tweedy, of Concord, and Mrs. Will Hunter, of Gladys to mourn his death. He was laid to rest in the family burying ground by the side of his wives.

The pall bearers were his sons and son-in-laws. The funeral was conducted by Rev. E. R. Crawley, D. G. Trent and Bolling Moore. The grave was covered with beautiful flowers. He leaves a large number of friends to mourn his death.

A friend, Bertha Tweedy

Riverside Farm-Thelma, the infant child of Mr. and Mrs. N. S. Joy, died last Wednesday morning and was buried at Union Hill Thursday afternoon at 3 o'clock. We extend our deepest sympathy to the bereaved parents in their loss.

August 6, 1920

Naruna-Mrs. Blanche Scott Carwile died last Saturday at her home near Naruna, aged 89 years, and was buried at the family burying ground Sunday afternoon. The funeral services were conducted by Rev. J. B. Lavinder assisted by Rev. D. G. Trent. She leaves the following children; Calvin, Glover and Booker Carwile, of Concord; Mrs. D. G. Foster, of Gladys; Mrs. W. J. Woodall, Misses Susie and Nannie Carwile of Naruna. She is also survived by nine grandchildren and fourteen great grandchildren. Her husband died about 20 years ago.

August 13, 1920

Mrs. Blanch C. Carwile died on Saturday night, July 31, at her home near Naruna, aged 89 years, and was buried at the family burying ground Sunday afternoon. The funeral services were conducted by Rev. D. G. Trent, assisted by Rev. J. B. Lavinder. She leaves the following children: Floyd Carwile, of Concord; Mrs. D. W. Foster, of Gladys; Mrs. W. J. Woodall; Booker, Glover, Calvin, Nannie and Susan Ann, of Naruna. She was a daughter of Ligon Holt and wife of M. S. Carwile, who died twenty years ago.

Red Farm-We are sorry to hear of the death of Mr. Suddith's little child, which died last Thursday evening.

Ruth Virginia Suddith-Thursday night, August 5th, at 10 o'clock the death angel visited the home of Mr. and Mrs. C. I. Suddith and took from them their precious baby girl, Ruth, aged 2 years and 2 months. She had been ill only 8 days. All that skilled physicians and loving hands could do was done, but God knew best. He had put her here only to be a pattern, never to live and toil in this world. Weep not, dear parents, God doeth all things well. He had a place in glory for her which no other could fill. He took that little bud from its earthly home and carried it to heaven to be an angel, pure and sweet.
She leaves to mourn their loss father, mother, brother and sister. She was laid to rest in Ebenezar cemetery Friday afternoon. The

funeral services were conducted by Rev. A. M. Padgett, of Gladys.
Mother put away the little dresses
The little darling use to wear
She will need them on earth, never,
She has climbed the golden stair.
She is with the happy angels
And we long for her sweet kiss,
Where her little feet are waiting
In the realm of perfect bliss.
Yes, mother, put away her little play things
Weep with mother's pearly tears
For we shall miss our darling Ruth,
All the coming weary years.
Kiss the little curly tresses
Cut from her bright golden hair
Do the angels kiss our darling
In the realms so bright and fair?
Oh! we pray to meet our darling
For that long sweet embrace,
Where our precious ones are waiting
When we meet them face to face.
A Friend

August 20, 1920

Drowned in Swollen River-While on his way home near Six-Mile-Bridge, in this county, last Wednesday night, Lafayette Watkins Drinkard attempted to ford a creek which had become swollen by heavy rains. The buggy was upset and the young man drowned. The first information that something was wrong was when the horse came to a neighbors home next morning wearing the remains of the broken harness. Search of the stream disclosed the broken buggy some distance below the ford, and on Saturday the body was found about two miles further down the stream. The coroners inquest rendered a verdict of accidental drowning, He was 18 years of age and a member of Indian Hill Methodist church. He is survived by his parents Mr. and Mrs. L. W. Drinkard, and five brothers, Henry, Russell, Raymond, Edward and Arthur.

The Death Angel visited the home of Rev. and Mrs. W. I. Hall, in Halifax county August 13, and called home their loving sister, Mrs. Fannie Dalton, age 66. She had been in ill health for six years. She is survived by two sisters and one brother as follows: Mrs. W. I. Hall, Mrs. A. A. Allen and Mr. R. L. Smith. She was loving and kind to everybody and will be greatly missed. The remains were laid to rest in the family burying ground Saturday.

Card of Thanks-Mr. and Mrs. S. P. Brown wish to thank the friends of the neighborhood for their many kindnesses shown to them during the illness and death of their baby.
"He gathered the little children round about Him and blessed them". He called little Shirley from us Monday night about 8:30 o'clock. Altho we miss him and it seems hard to have him go, we know that he, too, is blessed.

August 27, 1920

Mike-Mr. B. G. Fore, of near Chap, but well known in this neighborhood committed suicide last Saturday morning by shooting himself with a shot gun. He was buried Sunday afternoon at the old burying ground at George Haynes' near Red House.

Evol-Mrs. W. M. Hines and children and Mr. and Mrs. S. I. Burch and son of Dendron, Va., spent a few days at Evol last week, having come to attend the burial of their sister, Mrs. J. C. Sampson, of Columbus, Ohio. Mrs. Sampson, formerly Miss Ida Crawley, eldest daughter of A. B. Crawley, of Evol, was operated on in a Columbus hospital on August 9th and died August 16th. Her daughter, Miss Gracie Moore, who had been spending the summer at Evol, also her sister, Mrs. W. A. Gwaltney, of Dendrone, reached her bedside a few hours before her death. She was laid to rest in beautiful Spring Hill Cemetery Lynchburg. Her mound was covered by a profusion of lovely flowers. Her husband, J. C. Sampson, Mr. and Mrs. P. T. Sampson and her daughter by a former marriage, Miss Gracie Moore, of Columbus, Ohio, and her son, Maurice Moore, of Detroit, Michigan and Mrs. Gwaltney, accompanied the remains to Lynchburg.

September 3, 1920

Winchester- Benjamin Smallwood, aged 58 retired Clarke county farmer, committed suicide, it is said , by shooting through the heart with a shortgun, while in the garden at his home in Berryville, probably discharging the gun with a cane. Relatives and neighbors hearing the shot found him dead. Worry over money matters was the probable cause.

Riverside Farm -The death angel entered the home of Mr. and Mrs. Volney Childress last Saturday and took from them their infant son. Their other children are ill with the whooping cough.

Perth-We was sorry to hear of the death of Mr. Jim Robert Davis' little baby, who died Saturday before last and its mother had been dead only two months.

September 17, 1920

Dies from Effect of Wound-Richmond-Raymond Baker, of Dillwyn, Buckingham county, shot several days ago by Wyatt Pendleton, when Baker was escorting a young girl from church, died Thursday from the effects of the shot. He has been under treatment in a local hospital since the day of the shooting. The body will be taken back to his former home for burial. Just what reason there may have been for the shooting is not known, unless it was that Pendleton was of a jealous nature. The affair occasioned much talk in the community, where the young man lived and he was well and favorably known.

Mr. J. A. Midkiff, who lived at Elder's Store, and who had been in a South Boston hospital for treatment for several days, died suddenly of heart failure in the hospital Tuesday morning, September 14 at 6:30. He was buried Wednesday at the old family burying ground near Younger's Store in Halifax county. The funeral services were conducted by Rev. G. C. Duncan. The pallbearers were his nephews: H. T., W. A., and J. B. Younger, William and Guy Midkiff and Tom Vernon.
Mr. Midkiff is survived by his mother, wife, and five children, one sister and six brothers, one of whom is Mr. W. L. Midkiff, of

Brookneal.

In the Memory of Father-In the memory of our husband and father who passed from this old stormy life to a home that's brighter than here, on June 23, 1920, at his home near Perth. All that loving hands, kind physicians and friends could do could not stay the cold hand of death. He was a faithful member of Clover Bottom Church, one that was so successful through life, so kind and loving to all. He was especially devoted to his wife and children. So many sweet and comforting words have been spoken to us in this hour of trouble of praise of his noble and loyal life. Yet the way seems so dark here without him, yes we miss him more than words can ever express. But we feel comforted to know that he is enjoying that sweet and everlasting peace which nothing can destroy. But some day we hope to meet and clasp hands with him once more. We submit to God's holy will, believing that he is too good to do wrong and too wise too make a mistake. He leaves to mourn his loss, wife, five children, two brothers and one sister and a host of heart broken friends. This loss to us is but his eternal gain. The Lord giveth and the Lord taketh away. Blessed be his name. His first wife preceeded him to the grave just 2 year and four months ago.
Silently the shades of evening
Gathered round our lonely door,
Silently they bring before us
A face we shall see no more.
How such holy memories cluster
Like the stars when storms are past
Pointing up to that fair heaven
We may hope to gain at last.
A few more years shall roll,
A few more seasons come,
And we will be with those
Who rest asleep within the tomb.
A few more waves shall shall beat
On this wild rocky shore,
And we too shall be where tempests cease
And surges roll no more.
Written by his loving wife and children

September 24, 1920

Mrs. Willie Ann Daniel died last Friday at the home of her son, Archer, and was buried at Falling church Saturday. Mrs. Daniel was quite old and had been in poor health for some time. She was the mother of quite a large family among whom are C. S., Luther, John and Archer, all of Brookneal. The funeral service was conducted by Rev. W. F. Fisher.

Died at his home near Aspen, Va., September 4th, 1920, George G. Reese, aged 33 years. He leaves a wife, one child and four sisters and a host of friends and loved ones to mourn his death.
He was quietly laid to rest at Bethel church on Sunday September 5th. The funeral services were conducted by Rev. F. M. Ryburn, and D. C. Puckett, A. G. Cross, Harry Morris, Haywoood Hamilton, Edd Smith and Frank Clydus acted as pallbearers.
The death of an old person is like the falling leaves in autumn, for a time it seems desolate, but soon the sadness and gloom are driven away by the hope of spring time, the resurrection of a new period of life.
However, when a bright young life in the early spring of its existance is taken away it is different. In the presence of unfolding maturing life all around, it is hard to realize that this young life so rich in promise is gone never to return.
Dearest George, thou hast left us,
And your loss we deeply feel;
But it's God that has beret us,
He can all our corrows (sorrows) heal.
Yes, we miss his smiling presence,
When we see his vacant chair,
But in heaven I hope to meet you,
There will be no parting there.
His wife

Crosby-Our deepest sympathy goes out to the bereaved family of Mr. Allie Midkiff, who died in a South Boston hospital last Tuesday.

The funeral of Mrs. Willie Ann Daniel, of Brookneal, was conducted at Falling church last Saturday afternoon and her remains were laid to rest in Falling cemetery.

October 1, 1920

In Memoriam-In sad, but loving remembrance of my dear
husband, Charlie E. Joy, who departed this life one year ago today,
Sept. 23, 1919.
Dearest husband, you have left me,
Left the home you loved so well,
But someday I hope to meet you
And together we shall dwell.
In the grave-yard calmly sleeping,
Where the flowers nod and wave,
Lies the one I loved so dearly,
In his lone and silent grave.
And the midnight stars are beaming
O'er that lone and silent grave,
Where in sleep that knows no dreaming
Lies the one we could not save.
He has crossed the veil of shadows,
He has crossed the narrow sea,
And beyond the crystal river
He is waiting now for me.
How we miss your gentle footsteps,
How we miss your dear, sweet face,
How we miss you 'round the fireside,
Miss, you, dear, in every place.
Gone thou art, but not forgotten,
But we hope to meet some day,
And together we shall dwell
In that land of bliss always.
Written by his wife, Mrs. Bessie Joy

Gladys-Mrs. Mary Watson Cabell died at the home of her
daughter, Mrs. A. M. Pagett, of this place, Sunday afternoon at
3:30.

October 8, 1920

In Memoriam-In the memory of my dear husband who died

October 12, 1918, and my darling daughter who died June 12, 1920.
Both precious to our hearts, have gone;
The voices we loved are stilled.
Their place, made vacant in our home
Can nevermore be filled.
Our Father in his wisdom called
The boon his love had given,
And though on earth their bodies lie,
Their souls are safe in heaven.
Mrs. S. O. Dunn

October 15, 1920

Killed by Live Wire-Roanoke, Oct. 11.- Mosby Hurt 16 years old, son of John W. Hurt is dead as a result of being shocked by a live wire at the fair grounds Saturday afternoon. The boy was taken to the Jefferson Hospital immediately after being shocked, but he never regained consciousness, dying within an hour after the accident.

October 22, 1920

Mr. Joe Charlesworth died Saturday morning while sitting at the breakfast table. He had been apparently well until a few minutes before the end came. Mr. Charlesworth was an Englishman by birth, coming of this country many years ago. He is survived by his widow, who was Miss Lucy Daniel. He was a member of Beulah M.E. Church, and his remains were laid to rest there on Sunday afternoon.

October 29, 1920

Aspen-The infant child of Mr. and Mrs. J. W. Martin died last Thursday night after being ill for some time.

The little daughter of Mr. and Mrs. W. N. Williams, who had been sick for quite a while, died Wednesday morning. The remains were buried at the Methodist church at Mt. Carmel.

Mrs. Amanda McKinney has returned to her home in Lynchburg after being called at the death of her little grandchild.

Mrs. D. A. Hancock died at the home near Madisonville, on Oct. 16, 1920, in the 71st year of her age, her death being caused from heart trouble. She had been in feeble health for several years and bore her afflictions and suffering with patience. She was a loyal member of Rough Creek Presbyterian church and was loved by all who knew her. She will be greatly missed in the community and by a large circle of friends.

Her remains were laid to rest in the family burying ground at her home, the funeral services being conducted by her pastor, Rev. F. M. Ryburn, assisted by Rev. A. J. Ponton. The hymns that were sung were, "Asleep in Jesus," "Shall we gather at the river," "Abide with me," and Oh, think of the home over there." She is survived by her husband, Mr. D. A. Hancock, and the following children: Mr. J. W. Hancock, of Tams, W.Va., Mr. D. M. Hancock, of near Red House, Mr. H. M. Hancock, of Rough Creek; Mr. Douglas Hancock, of Ashville, Ky.; Mrs. L. S. Shorter, of Madisonville; Mrs. W. W. LeGrande, of Crewe; Mrs. J. D. Elliotte, of Wren; Miss Bessie Hancock and Mrs. O. L. Snell of Rough Creek.

November 5, 1920

Mr. and Mrs. Fulton White attended the funeral of Mr. J. F. M. White at Cullen Tuesday. He was Mr. White's father and has spent a good portion of his time in our town.

Mr. J. F. M. White aged seventy-four years died in a hospital at Petersburg on Monday after a brief illness, although he had been in poor health for some time. The remains were brought to his old home near Cullen for interment on Tuesday, the funeral services being conducted by Rev. F. M. Ryburn, assisted by Rev. Keys at Oak View Presbyterian church, of which the deceased was a member. The pallbearers were the four sons and two son-in-laws of the deceased, as follows: W. F. White, of Brookneal; J. C. White, of Winding Golf, W.Va.,; J. M. White, of Newport News; C.C. White, of Victoria; L.G. Leigh, of Petersburg and W. S. Barksdale of Cullens. The flowers were borne by his two brother-in-laws, Wm. and James Henderson and two friends A. L. Landers and Jas. Leigh. Besides the above mentioned sons, Mr. White is survived by his wife and seven daughters; Mmes. W. S. Barksdale, of Cullen; T. W. Balloa , of Richmond; L. G. Leigh, of Petersburg; H. B. Turner, of Winding Gulf, W.Va.; and Misses Fannie, Virginia and Winnie White. Also one brother, Mr. John White, of Statesville, Va., and one sister, Mrs. Sallie Ann Bohanon, of Pittsylvania county.

November 12, 1920

Mr. Ed M. Smith who was a native of Brookneal and a brother of Mr. P. P. Smith, was killed at Monroe last Friday at about 6 o'clock pm by being mashed between the engine and first coach of a train on the Southern Railway. Mr. Smith was 45 years of age and is survived by his widow, three children and four brothers.

The remains of Guy McDowell, who died in France were intered Arlington Friday of last week. His father, Mr. Charles McDowell, brother E. G. and sister, Mrs. L. H. Coleman, attended the burial.

Green Hill Road-Mrs. S. W. East received a letter from her son, J. B. East, announcing the death of his little daughter, Mary on Nov. 2nd.

November 19, 1920

Miss Lucy Rodenhizer, daughter of the late D. K. Rodenhizer, died at her home in Danville Sunday, Nov. 15th, after a long illness. She was born in Brookneal, but had lived in Danville since 1881, being 59 years old at the time of her death.

Mr. Walter Francis died at his home near Evol Wednesday morning, Nov. 17, at 2:30 o'clock after a prolonged illness, aged 61 years. His remains were interred at the old Martin burying ground Thursday afternoon, the funeral services were conducted by Rev. D. G. Trent.
Mr. Francis is survived by his wife and one daughter, besides three brothers, R. F., of near Stovall, J. W., of Long Island, and W. L., of near Nathalie.

The little infant son of Mr. and Mrs. Will P. Holt died Saturday and was buried at Falling River Cemetery Sunday afternoon. They have the sympathy of many friends.

In Memoriam--In loving remembrance of my dear brother, Paul W. Landrum, who left us one year ago, November 19, 1919.
Today recalls sad memories
Of our brother gone to rest
And those who think of him most
Are those who loved him best.
Sister Laura

November 26, 1920

The body of Mrs. W. A. Jones, who died at Madison Heights, was brought to Gladys last Saturday and buried in the cemetery at Kedron Baptist church, of which she was a member. The funeral service was conducted by Rev. Mr. Mintx, of Madison Heights and Rev. A. M. Padgett, of Gladys.

Evol-Mr. Walter Francis, mention of whose death was made in these columns last week, will be greatly missed. He was a very popular man as was attested by the large gathering and the floral offerings at his burial. Your correspondent has known him a number of years and was a frequent visitor in his home and we have never heard him speak a harmful word of any one. His wife and daughter have the sympathy of a host of friends.
Mr. Chris Martin and daughter, Mrs. Guy Creasy, and Mr. Eddie Francis, of Richmond, who came to attend the burial of Mr. Walter Francis on last Thursday have returned to their home.

Raymond Hunter attended the burial of his aunt, Mrs. Button Jones, who died at Madison Heights on Wednesday of last week and was buried at Kedron on Friday.

Bell Glade Farm-We were very sorry to hear of the death of Mr. Walter Francis.

Bethlehem-Mrs. Walker Putney died Monday morning at 5

151

o'clock. Interment took place at Spring Creek Baptist church Tuesday. She leaves a husband and three sons, Dr. Lewis Putney, of Staunton, Mr. Charles Putney, of the Medical College at Richmond and Mr. Hansford Putney. All were at her bedside when the end came. Mrs. Putney was truly a good woman, to know her was to love her, ever gentle and affectionate. She will be surely missed in her home as well as by her numerous friends. We wish to extend our sympathy to the bereaved ones.

Card of Thanks-We wish to thank our neighbors and friends for their many acts of kindness and words of sympathy and tended to us in the illness and death of our husband and father, Walter Francis.
His wife and Daughter

December 3, 1920

Miss Elvira A. Bates, aged about 60, died suddenly at her home near Crystal Hill, Friday night about 8 p.m. She had been active in household duties along with other members of the family during the day, and went to her room about 6 o'clock. No one had heard her complain and therefore none knew that there was anything wrong with her. Her sister, retiring later, found her in a dying condition. Medical aid was called but she was dead before the arrival of the physician. Her death was attributed to appoplexy. The remains were interred at 3 p.m., Saturday in the home burying ground, the funeral service being conducted by Rev. Mr. Marsh. Miss Bates is survived by two brothers, Wm. M., of Brookneal and J.M., who resides at the old home, also two sisters, Misses Virginia and May, both residing at the old home near Crystal Hill. Mr. and Mrs. Wm. Bates, Sr. and Mr. and Mrs. Thornton Bates, of Brookneal, attended the funeral.

Evol-Mrs. Buck Fore was notified last week if the death of her little nephew, Abraham Mayberry. He accidently shot himself while alone in the woods and was dead when found. He was only 10 years old. His parents live near Spout Springs and are deaf mutes.

In Memoriam-In loving remembrance of our beloved son, Dorsie

Jordan, who departed this life on Dec. 2, 1918.
God needed another dear one
To join his shining hand
So he sent an angel down
To clasp our darling's hand
Yet again we hope to meet him
When life's short days have fled
And in heaven may we greet him
Where no farewell tears are shed.
A loved one from us is gone,
A voice we loved is stilled
A place is vacant in our home
Which never can be filled.
His Mother

On Nov. 25, 1920, Mr. G. C. Jackson, of Alton, Va., aged 70 years passed from this old stormy life to a home that's brighter than here. All that loving hands, kind physicians and friends could do could not stay the cold hand of death. He had been a faithful member of Alton Baptist church for thirty years, and was especially devoted to his wife and children. So many sweet and comforting words have been spoken to us in this hour of trouble in praise of his noble and loyal life. Yes, we miss him more than words can ever express.

His last words were, "I am ready to go." But some day we hope to meet and clasp hands with him once more. He leaves to mourn his loss his wife, three children, Mr. M. T. Jackson, of Alton, Mr. W. H. Jackson and Mrs. O. L. Snead, of Brookneal. He is also survived by thirteen grandchildren and three great-grandchildren, besides a host of heart-broken friends. The Lord giveth and the Lord taketh away, Blessed be the name of the Lord.

His remains were interred in the Alton cemetery on the day following his death. The pallbearers were George Cliborn, Andrew Turner, Willie Walker, Robert Turner, Dabner Warren and Jim Pulliam. The flower bearers were his two granddaughters and other near relatives, Mrs. Johnnie Walker, Misses Ola Jackson, Lottie Morris, Estelle Reaves, Vick Walker, Evelin Gravett and Shina Pulliam.

One that loved him.

December 10, 1920

Oakdale (Charlotte county) -Mr. and Mrs. Sidney Reynolds were called to Rocky Mount last Friday on account of the death of Mr. Douglas Hunt, brother of Mrs. Reynolds.

December 17, 1920

Smith, the son of Mr. and Mrs. Artie Tweedy, of near Concord, died Sunday, Dec. 5th at 10 o'clock from bronical pneumonia. He was operated on in Charlottesville about three months ago about three months ago, after which he never recovered. He was fourteen years of age, and a member of New Chapel Baptist church. He was laid to rest at the church Monday afternoon at three o'clock, the funeral being conducted by Rev.W. S. Royall. "In The Sweet Bye and Bye," "On Jordan Stormy Bank," "Shall we Gather at the River," and "Wait and Murmur Not" were sung. He is survived by his parents and four sisters. Smith was loved by all who knew him and always had a smiling face. A large crowd assembled to pay their last respects.

December 24, 1920

In Memoriam-In loving rembrance of my beloved niece, Gertrude Richardson who departed this life on Dec. 14, 1918.
God needed another dear one
To join his shining hand
So he sent an angel gown
To clasp dear Gertrude's hand
The silver cord was broken
Brightness left the day
The spring turned back to winter
When Gertrude went away
Shall we listen to Gertrude's voice
Clasp her hand or kiss her brow
Will the circle be unbroken
When we gather over there?
Her aunt

December 31, 1920

Mr. James H. Rush, a native of Appomattox county and brother of Mr. L. W. Rush, of Brookneal, died at his home in Lynchburg Monday morning, Dec. 27, aged 62 years. He is survived by his widow, one daughter and ten sons. His body was buried in the Presbyterian cemetery in Lynchburg Tuesday afternoon.

Three Forks-Mr. and Mrs. J. H. Dawson were called to Pittsylvania county on the 20th to attend the burial of Mrs. Dawson's niece, Mrs. Josie Hodnett of Keeling, Va. Also while out there they visited Mr. Dawsons sister, Mrs. Haywood Dalton who is very ill at Ringgold.

Booker T. Harris, a colored boy about fourteen years of age, whose home was at Middledtown, accidentally shot and killed himself Wednesday afternoon while hunting. He had crawled through a wire fence and endeavored to pull the gun through after him when the trigger hung on the fence causing the gun to be discharged, the entire load striking the boy on the left side just above the heart and causing almost instant death. His only companion was another small colored boy. Justice J. F. Peterson viewed the remains and decided that an inquest was unnecessary. The boy was the son of Walter Gray Harris.

Mrs. Mattie Johnson died in her home in Cheatham Thursday morning Dec. 30th, after a prolonged illness from pneumonia. Mrs. Johnson was a sister of Mrs. M. J. Wickliffe, of Brookneal, and is pleasantly in membered (remembered) by many friends in this section.

Abbot, Frazer Thornton 5/23/1919
Adams, Mrs. C. C. (Mittie Francis)
6/8/1917
Adams, Amanda Jane (Mrs. R.E.)
2/27/1920
Adams, Amanda J. 3/5/1920
Adams, C. C. 3/19/1920
Allen, A. A. 7/2/1920
Anderson, Mrs. Henry 1/2/1920
Angel, Napoleon 12/20/1918
Asher, Alexander 6/2/1916
Atkins, Emory 1/24/1919
Averette, Billie 6/27/1919
Averette, Mr. and Mrs. W.W.-son
7/18/1919
Bailey, Courtney Berkley 9/5/1919
Bailey, Courtney Berkley
9/19/1919
Baker, Raymond 9/17/1920
Baldwin, Elizabeth Langhorne
4/23/1920
Barrett, Albert and son 7/27/1917
Bass, Capt. W. A. 5/7/1920
Bates, Elvira A. 12/3/1920
Bennett, W.R. 10/3/1919
Bentley, Edward 8/1/1919
Bently, Alfred 5/10/1918
Berkley, Mrs. Woodson (Emma
Jackson) 7/12/1918
Berkley, Mary Smith 11/8/1918
Blanks, Mr. Ernest-infant son
7/13/1917
Blanks, Royal Herbert 8/10/1917
Bohannon, James 5/10/1918
Bradner, Mrs. 1/18/2018
Bradshaw, R. R. 4/2/1920
Bray, Tom 11/2/1917
Brewer, Mae 9/20/1918
Brewer, May 9/27/1918
Brooks, Fannie (Mrs. D.N.)
1/11/1918
Brooks, Mrs. D.N. 1/18/1918
Brooks, Fanny (Mrs. D.N.)
1/25/1918
Brooks, Fannie 3/29/1918
Brown, Jane 10/13/1916
Brown, Mary 2/15/1918
Brown, Mr. and Mrs. S. P.-baby
8/20/1920

Burks, Mrs. R.D. 10/5/1917
Burks, Lt. J. Beverly 8/1/1919
Burton, Zora Elizabeth 8/25/1916
Burton, Zora Bailey 11/10/1916
Bustard, Mrs. John, (Vina Clark)
12/15/1916
Cabaniss, John W. 7/19/1918
Cabell, Mary Watson 10/1/1920
Cardwell, Thomas 4/27/1917
Cardwell, Jack, Jr. 12/5/1919
Cardwell, Jack 12/5/1919
Carey, Lacy 9/5/1919
Carey, Lacy 9/19/1919
Carr, R. Bascom 3/8/1918
Carter, Mr. and Mrs. Cleveland-son
11/21/1919
Carwile, Emette 2/2/1917
Carwile, Pearl Helen, (Mrs. Luther)
10/25/1918
Carwile, Pearl 11/8/1918
Carwile, Mrs. Pierce 2/28/1919
Carwile, Robert 3/28/1919
Carwile, Lizzie 7/18/1919
Carwile, Mrs. 6/11/1920
Carwile, Blanche Scott 8/6/1920
Carwile, Blanch C. 8/13/1920
Chaney, Annie 7/27/1917
Charlesworth, Joe 10/22/1920
Childress, Mr. and Mrs. S.M.-child
11/29/1918
Childress, Mr. and Mrs. Volney-
son 9/3/1920
Clark, Pub 2/11/1916
Clark, Hon. Thos. B. 7/18/1919
Clay, Stephen M. 10/4/1918
Clay, Charles Moorman 6/6/1919
Clowdis, Mrs. W.-baby 7/13/1917
Clowdis, Fred 7/19/1918
Coates, Henry 5/5/1916
Coates, Mr. & Mrs. C.W.-child
7/20/1917
Coates, Emma Thornton 8/1/1919
Coates, Mrs. W.H. (Eula Carr)
2/20/1920
Cocke, Martha A. (Mrs. Lewallen)
11/16/1917
Colbert, Mrs. W.D. 1/31/1919
Coleman, Will-father 6/4/1920
Collins, Samuel B. 10/31/1919

Compton, Mr. and Mrs. Obie-infant 3/12/1920
Conthran, Samuel B. 3/12/1920
Cook, Temple 2/8/1918
Cook, Helen 12/12/1919
Cooke, St. George H. 5/26/1916
Cothran, Lizzie 2/18/1916
Cothran, Mary Elizabeth 2/25/1916
Cothran, Mrs. E.H. 1/12/1917
Covington, John 7/13/1917
Covington, Mr. and Mrs. Thornton-daughter 6/14/1918
Cox, Mrs. Nate (Mrs. Jordan) 11/16/1917
Crane, Robert E. 7/27/1917
Crank, C.E. 5/12/1916
Crank, Sallie Bell 1/16/1920
Crews, Mamie 8/31/1917
Crews, Thompson 1/24/1919
Crews, Isaac H. 8/22/1919
Crews, Isaac Henry 8/29/1919
Crickenburger, Nora-sister-in-law 2/20/1920
Cumbie, R.R. 4/18/1919
Cyrus, Mrs. Oscar 6/11/1920
Cyrus, Mrs. Ady 6/11/1920
Dalton, Fannie 8/20/1920
Daniel, C.S.-child 5/18/1917
Daniel, Mrs. William 3/1/1918
Daniel, Bettie 12/27/1918
Daniel, Mrs. J.W. 12/27/1918
Daniel, Bettie Mays, (Mrs. J.W.) 1/31/1919
Daniel, Willie Ann 9/24/1920
Daulton, John 11/15/1918
Daulton, Mrs. C.J. 1/10/1919
Davenport, Gette 2/13/1920
Davidson, Lula 12/20/1918
Davidson, Lula Christine 12/27/1918
Davis, Lelia 12/28/1917
Davis, R. Bailey 5/28/1920
Davis, Mrs. Jim Robert 7/2/1920
Davis, Jim Robert-child and mother 9/3/1920
DeJarnette, Mary Edness 6/6/1919
DeJarnette, Willie (Mrs. Dock) 5/14/1920
Dews, Garnet 3/5/1920

Dickerson, Arthur 8/4/1917
Dickerson, T.E 10/12/1917
Dickerson, Tom 10/12/1917
Douglas, John L., Jr. 1/16/1920
Douglas, John L., Jr. 1/23/1920
Drinkard, Lafayette Watkins 8/20/1920
Driscoll, Arsella Virginia 12/1/1916
Duff, David 6/2/1916
Dunivant, L.W. 8/24/1917
Dunn, Shirley O. 10/18/1918
Dunn, Mrs. Hitchie 1/24/1919
Dunn, S.O. 10/8/1920
Dyer, Thomas 3/10/1916
East, John W. 7/9/1920
East, Mary 11/12/1920
Edmunds, Mrs. Jim 11/30/1917
Elam, Mrs. John, (Lizzie Nowlin) 10/19/1917
Elam, Mitchell-child 7/19/1918
Elder, Andrew 7/21/1916
Elder, Martha A. (Mrs. Lewallen) 5/11/1917
Elder, Mrs. Wesley 9/28/1917
Elder, David T. 4/26/1918
Elder, Emma-husband 4/26/1918
Elder, David T. 5/3/1918
Elder, C.W. 12/20/1918
Elder, C.W. 1/3/1919
Elder, Elijah T. 12/26/1919
Elder, R. O. 1/9/1920
Elliott, Hugh 1/7/1916
Elliott, H. N. 1/14/1916
Elliott, Ethel Roden, (Mrs. W. S.) 2/21/1919
Elliotte, Mrs. W.S. 2/14/1919
Elmore, W.T. 9/1/1916
Epes, Philip 3/22/1918
Evans, Guss 1/12/1917
Evans, Edward G. 5/17/1918
Ewel, Aunt Sue 4/2/1920
Farmer, William 3/1/1918
Farmer, W.B. 3/8/1918
Farmer, W.B. 3/22/1918
Farris, Rev. H.H. and Wife 1/31/1919
Ferguson, W. D. 4/2/1920
Fisher, John 8/23/1918

Fitch, Mr. and Mrs. Booker-
daughter 3/19/1920
Fitch, Alma 3/19/1920
Fitch, Alma 3/26/1920
Fore, Lizzie O. 6/2/1916
Fore, Mr. B. G. 8/27/1920
Foster, Charles H. 8/4/1916
Foster, Mrs.T. L.(Dollie A.
Woolridge) 3/9/1917
Foster, Mrs. T. L. 3/9/1917
Foster, Chas. H. 11/23/1917
Foster, Clayton L. 12/28/1917
Foster, Neal 2/21/1919
Foster, G.W. 6/27/1919
Foster, Victoria (Mrs. J.Y.)
8/8/1919
Foster, Henry Lee 9/5/1919
Foster, Henry Lee 9/19/1919
Francis, Cornelia 2/20/1920
Francis, Mary 5/28/1920
Francis, Walter 11/19/1920
Francis, Walter 11/26/1920
Franklin,Tom 2/6/1920
Gaines, T. N. 3/15/1918
Gilliam, Mrs. W. F. 7/21/1916
Gilliam, Mr. W. F.-wife 7/28/1916
Gilliam, James R. 5/18/1917
Gilliam, Jane Hamlet 7/28/1916
Gilliland, Dwight 8/10/1917
Ginther, Mary L., (Mrs. W.H.)
12/21/1917
Glass, Earlie 1/2/1920
Guthrie, Leonard 3/16/1917
Guthrie, Leonard 3/30/1917
Guthrie, Tommy 10/12/1917
Guthrie, Richard 3/1/1918
Guthrie, Mrs. Lawrence
10/10/1919
Haden, Socrates 2/21/1919
Hamlet, "Aunt" Lucy 7/27/1917
Hamlet, Sidney 6/18/1920
Hancock, Carrie Olivia 2/1/1918
Hancock, Carrie 2/1/1918
Hancock, Alphonzo 1/17/1919
Hancock, Mrs. D. A. 10/29/1920
Hankley, Mrs. John 6/27/1919
Hannah, PM. 8/22/1919
Harper, William 8/16/1918
Harper, Mrs. M.J. 2/6/1920

Harper, Mary Jane 2/6/1920
Harper, Mrs. Henry 3/19/1920
Harper, Carie Holmes Elder (Mrs.
Henry) 3/26/1920
Harris, Booker T. 12/31/1920
Harvey, Martha J. 2/4/1916
Harvey, H.W. 6/23/1916
Harvey, Henry W. 6/23/1916
Harvey, Mattie, (Mrs. Wyatt)
4/19/1918
Harvey, Mattie, (Mrs. W.W.)
4/26/1918
Harvey, Mrs. Wyatt 5/24/1918
Harvey, Walter 9/20/1918
Harvey, Charles W. 4/4/1919
Harvey, Uncle Wyat 2/6/1920
Harvey, Ben 7/9/1920
Henderson, Mr. 2/25/1916
Henderson, Edgar 5/19/1916
Henderson, E.H. 5/19/1916
Henderson, Edgar H. 5/18/1917
Henderson, Marion 5/14/1920
Hendrick, Martha W. 6/16/1916
Hendricks, Mrs. J. 6/9/1916
Henry, Dr. Thomas Stanhope
2/13/1920
Hester, Mrs. A. S. 9/26/1919
Hill, Jamie 9/7/1917
Hill, Cindy 8/23/1918
Hodnett, Josie 12/31/1920
Holloway, L. O. 4/23/1920
Holloway, L. O. 4/30/1920
Holt, Henry Calvin 6/23/1916
Holt, S. T.-son 6/23/1916
Holt, Henry Calvin 7/7/1916
Holt, Malcolm Edward 12/8/1916
Holt, Mr. and Mrs. Leslie-daughter
7/11/1919
Holt, Mr. and Mrs. Will P.
11/19/1920
Howard, Mr. 2/20/1920
Hubbard, Ellen 3/8/1918
Hubbard, Mrs. S.C. 2/7/1919
Hubbard, John William 2/27/1920
Hudson, J. J. 11/7/1919
Hunt, Mrs.-baby boy 6/8/1917
Hunt, Sallie 2/1/1918
Hunt, Douglas 12/10/1920

Hunter, Mr. and Mrs. John E.-baby 10/24/1919
Hunter, Eugene 12/5/1919
Hurt, Taw 10/12/1917
Hurt, Ora Bessie, (Mrs. T.W.) 5/10/1918
Hurt, Bessie 5/10/1918
Hurt, Hubbard Monroe 3/12/1920
Hurt, Mosby 10/15/1920
Ingram, Mr. and Mrs. Boss 6/20/1919
Ingram, Randolph 6/20/1919
Jackson, Cris 6/27/1919
Jackson, Elijah M. (Uncle Chris) 7/4/1919
Jackson, G.C. 12/3/1920
James, Joe 7/2/1920
Jenkins, J. Edward 9/8/1916
Jennings, Mr. & Mrs. Eulee-baby 2/2/1917
Jennings, John 11/30/1917
Jennings, Dick 5/3/1918
Jennings, Emily S. 8/16/1918
Johnson, Mrs. Juda 6/21/1918
Johnson, Martin 9/27/1918
Johnson, Bernard 12/27/1918
Johnson, "Aunt" Lettie Elisa 10/31/1919
Johnson, Agnes 3/19/1920
Johnson, Mattie 12/31/1920
Johnston, Henry Lee 11/3/1916
Jones, W.A. 7/19/1918
Jones, Button 7/26/1918
Jones, William A. 8/9/1918
Jones, R.H. 5/21/1920
Jones, Geo. W. 7/30/1920
Jones, Mrs. W. A. 11/26/1920
Jones, Mrs. Button 11/26/1920
Jordan, Nannie Blanche (Mrs. W.T.) 4/21/1916
Jordan, Fowler 11/30/1917
Jordan, Ora (Mrs. Claude) 3/1/1918
Jordan, Dorsie 12/6/1918
Jordan, Dorsey 12/13/1918
Jordan, Hamilton 12/27/1918
Jordan, Lillie 11/21/1919
Jordan, Lillian 11/28/1919
Jordan, Davis 4/2/1920

Jordan, Davis B. 4/9/1920
Jordan, Dorsie 12/3/1920
Joy, Mrs. L. H.(Lillie E. Sublett) 1/5/1917
Joy, Thelma 7/30/1920
Joy, Charlie E. 10/1/1920
Joy, Charlie 10/3/1919
Kersey, Wayland 7/12/1918
Kesler, R. L. 9/27/1918
Kinder, Mr. and Mrs.-baby 1/24/1919
Kittredge, Mrs. R. 1/16/1920
Klein, Hannah Alice 3/31/1916
Kline, Jacob Hoy 4/12/1918
Kline, Jake 4/19/1918
Lacy, Gertrude 2/8/1918
Landrum, Paul W. 11/28/1919
Landrum, Buck 5/28/1920
Landrum, Paul W. 11/19/1920
LaPrade, John C. 11/16/1917
Lash, W. L.-family 3/29/1918
Lash, George 3/29/1918
Lawson, James M. 2/4/1916
Lawson, Mrs. V. H. 6/9/1916
Lawson, Victoria Harvey 6/9/1916
Lawson, Victoria H. 10/27/1916
Lawson, Samuel A. 2/16/1917
Lawson, S. A. 2/23/1917
Layne, Geo. 10/4/1918
Lee, Mr. and Mrs. F. H.-infant 6/6/1919
Ligon, David B. 10/19/1917
Lipscomb, Mrs. Jeff 7/12/1918
Lipscomb, Labinda 2/20/1920
Lipscomb, Mrs. Tony-mother 3/12/1920
Little, Mrs. 11/8/1918
Lovelace, W. O. 4/6/1917
Loyd, Mrs. W. T. 4/2/1920
Maddox, Kathleen, (Mrs. S. L.) 10/31/1919
Maddox, Mrs. Sam 10/31/1919
Maddox, J. R. 2/20/1920
Maddox, Mrs. Nat 3/19/1920
Mann, Tom 8/31/1917
Mann, William Thomas 8/31/1917
Mann, Mrs. Daniel 4/9/1920
Marshall, David R. 2/16/1917
Marshall, John 11/30/1917

Marshall, John 12/7/1917
Marshall, Mrs. James 8/15/1919
Marshall, Lottie D. 9/5/1919
Marshall, Laura 2/13/1920
Martin, L. D. 6/9/1916
Martin, Grover H. 11/2/1917
Martin, Mr. and J. W.-child
10/29/1920
Martin, Glover 9/14/1917
Mason, Joe 10/5/1917
Mason, Mr and Mrs. Walter-child
3/1/1918
Mason, Leady 7/5/1918
Mason, Mrs. W. A. 12/27/1918
Mason, Florence   3/28/1919
Massey, Paul 11/15/1918
Mathews, Rev. John R. 1/31/1919
Mayberry, George 8/22/1919
Mayberry, Abraham 12/3/1920
Mays, R. Lit 2/13/1920
McCulloch, Jerry 6/13/1919
McCullough, J.E. 7/23/1920
McDowell, Grace 5/19/1916
McDowell, Guy 4/25/1919
McDowell, Guy 11/12/1920
McGann, Mrs. R. H. 10/10/1919
McIvor, Jim 9/28/1917
McKinley, Charlie 12/26/1919
McKinney, Mrs Reecy 1/16/1920
McKinney, Amanda-grandchild
10/29/1920
Merryman, Josiah 4/2/1920
Midkiff, J. A. 9/17/1920
Miles, Lena 11/1/1918
Miles, Mrs. Edward 11/1/1918
Minix, Mary 10/13/1916
Monroe, Susan 2/22/1918
Monroe, C. E. 11/22/1918
Monroe, Roxana 3/21/1919
Monroe, E. Gibbs 6/11/1920
Moon, Mrs. A. M 4/26/1918
Moon, Maude 12/27/1918
Moon, Herbert 1/24/1919
Moon, J. A.-mother 3/26/1920
Moore, Mrs. Esmond-son
12/5/1919
Morris, Thomas Edward 6/13/1919
Morrison, Mrs. Edwin 2/27/1920
Morton, Lizzie 11/8/1918

Morton, Mrs. Andrew 11/8/1918
Morton, W. R. 11/21/1919
Motomer, Reed 8/16/1918
Murphy, Billy 2/15/1918
Myers, Charles W. 3/24/1916
Nash, Mr. and Mrs. S. H.-baby
2/20/1920
Neal, Fannie 12/21/1917
Neil, John-4 children 3/26/1920
Nichols, J.R. 5/30/1919
Nichols, G.R. 6/6/1919
Patrick, Norman Robert 10/31/1919
Patrick, Henry Thomas 10/31/1919
Payne, Morris 9/13/1918
Pentecost, Mrs.Tommie 2/13/1920
Pentecost, Mrs. O. L. 2/20/1920
Phillips, Mrs. Massie 2/13/1920
Pillow, Mrs. Jack 5/25/1917
Poindexter, Mrs. J. B. 3/3/1916
Poindexter, Mattie 3/3/1916
Poole, Mr. and Mrs. John-child
10/18/1918
Price, Mrs. W. D. 4/18/1919
Price, William D.10/24/1919
Price, Carrington 1/25/1918
Price, Carrington 2/1/1918
Price, Tom 2/1/1918
Price, Carrington 2/8/1918
Puckett, Mary A. 12/22/1916
Puckett, Russell 9/12/1919
Puckette, Mrs. Dug 5/28/1920
Pugh, Wheeler 11/2/1917
Pugh, Marshall 3/12/1920
Pugh, Harvey 4/9/1920
Pulley, George E. 3/3/1916
Puryear, Nellie 3/5/1920
Puryear, Emma 3/12/1920
Putney, Mrs. Walker 11/26/1920
Ramsey, Mrs. John 5/28/1920
Randolph, Jack, Jr. 8/8/1919
Rasnick, Wm. S. 1/28/1916
Read, Dora 6/15/1917
Reese, George G. 9/24/1920
Reid, "Aunt" Lizzie (Mrs. L.R.)
1/18/1918
Reynolds, Willie (Mrs. Jim)
8/9/1918
Reynolds, Mary Willie 8/16/1918
Rice, William Anderson 4/20/1917

Rice, William R. 1/18/1918
Rice, Martha (Mrs. Joe) 2/22/1918
Rice, Mosby 5/24/1918
Rice, Mrs. J. 4/9/1920
Richardson, Gertrude 12/20/1918
Richardson, Gertrude 12/24/1920
Rickman, Mary (Mrs. J. Hubbard)
   10/5/1917
Ritcherson, Dewey 1/10/1919
Roach, W. T. 7/27/1917
Roakes, Lotty 3/24/1916
Robertson, Dr. Mott 8/22/1919
Robey, Harry C. 10/31/1919
Roby, Mrs. George 5/17/1918
Roby, George E. 11/15/1918
Rodenhizer, Lucy 11/19/1920
Rosser, Will 8/4/1917
Rudder, Leola Puckette 9/6/1918
Rudder, Mrs. J. T. 9/6/1918
Rudder, W. T. 9/6/1918
Rush, Lillie, (Mrs. Lacey W.)
   2/7/1919
Rush, James H. 12/31/1920
Sampson, Mrs. J.C. (Ida Crawley)
   8/27/1920
Saunders, Mr. & Mrs. Eva-infant
   daughter 10/5/1917
Scott, Francis Alexander 3/17/1916
Scott, Hubert 6/23/1916
Scott, W. B. 6/1/1917
Scott, William Bailey 6/1/1917
Scott, W. P. 5/10/1918
Scott, Mrs. Cabell Carrington,
   (Mary Pringle) 8/30/1918
Scott, Charles O. 4/4/1919
Scott, Mrs. Hudson 3/26/1920
Scott, Mrs. Hutson 4/2/1920
Scott, C. O. 4/9/1920
Scruggs, Hattie Taylor 7/13/1917
Scruggs, Thomas F. 11/16/1917
Seymore, Alex 10/19/1917
Shelton, Virginia 5/12/1916
Short, Whit 1/24/1919
Shotwell, William C. 10/24/1919
Simpson, Mrs. C. C. 9/5/1919
Smallwood, Benjamin 9/3/1920
Smith, Andrew 3/15/1918
Smith, Lucy, (Mrs. James)
   1/17/1919

Smith, Mrs. E. F. 1/24/1919
Smith, Ed M.   11/12/1920
Soyars, Rev. P. O. 10/18/1918
Soyars, Rev. P. O. 10/25/1918
Soyars, Rev. P.O. 11/22/1918
Spraggins, Watt 4/13/1917
Spurr, Andrew Lewis 3/29/1918
Stephens, R. H. 4/21/1916
Stevens, John Will 3/29/1918
Stevens, Mrs. H. E. 12/20/1918
Stout, Mrs. Allen M. 5/28/1920
Strictland, Mrs. C. B. 6/25/1920
Sublett, Jennie 12/13/1918
Sublett, Dan 12/13/1918
Sublett, Mrs. Richard 1/24/1919
Suddith, Bernice 7/18/1919
Suddith, Mr.–child 8/13/1920
Suddith, Ruth Virginia 8/13/1920
Swanson, Elizabeth Lyons(Mrs.
   Sen. Charles) 7/23/1920
Tanner, Walter Hugh 2/14/1919
Tanner, Mr. and Mrs. Willie-infant
   twin 4/23/1920
Taylor, Rosa Lee 2/25/1916
Taylor, J. P. 12/22/1916
Taylor, Harriet 12/5/1919
Terry, Joe 11/16/1917
Terry, Robert 2/8/1918
Terry, James M. 10/10/1919
Thomas, Mrs. Jim-granddaughter
   7/13/1917
Thomas, Zelia 3/22/1918
Threader, Mrs. Eugene 12/19/1919
Thurman, Henrietta Bennett
   8/1/1919
Tibbs, Lucy A. 2/21/1919
Tibbs, Mrs. 2/21/1919
Tibbs, Mrs. Robert 1/16/1920
Todd, Dr. A. S. 7/11/1919
Torrence, Wood 1/9/1920
Torrence, Mr. 1/23/1920
Trent, Luke M. 8/4/1916
Trent, Mr. and Mrs. Clem-infant
   3/12/1920
Tribble, Mrs. W. T. 2/22/1918
Tribble, Mrs. 3/1/1918
Tribble, Mrs. Whit 3/1/1918
Tribble, Mrs. W.T. 3/1/1918
Tribble, Lona-mother 3/7/1919

Tribble, W. T. 6/25/1920
Tuck, Albert-family 1/24/1919
Tucker, Hallie Marshall 11/30/1917
Tucker, Jim 5/16/1919
Tune, Miss Pattie 2/2/1917
Tune, Mrs. W.O.-brother-in-laws
children 11/8/1918
Tweedy, Mrs. Allen 5/10/1918
Tweedy, Mrs. Allen, (Trixy
Coates) 5/17/1918
Tweedy, Smith 12/17/1920
Tyree, R. A. 10/13/1916
Valley, Mrs. Louis 10/31/1919
Viar, Paul W. 3/19/1920
Virginia, Lena 12/20/1918
Wade, Julia 9/12/1919
Walker, Aunt Sally 11/30/1917
Walker, Pleasant R. 5/10/1918
Waller, Loyd 1/2/1920
Waller, Mr. and Mrs. Elmo-baby
1/23/1920
Waller, infant daughter 2/20/1920
Waller, Loyd 4/2/1920
Walthall, Miss Mary-mother
11/30/1917
Walthall, Napoleon-son 6/11/1920
Walthall, Louis 6/18/1920
Walton, Ethel, (Mrs. S. J.)
3/8/1918
Ware, Jeane B. 3/29/1918
Webb, J. M. 5/17/1918
Webb, Grace J.-family 5/17/1918
Webb, Tom-mother 5/7/1920
Webb, Grace J. (Mrs. J. M.)
5/7/1920
White, Mrs. 11/21/1919
White, J. F. M. 11/5/1920
Wickliffe, Mrs. M. J. 5/12/1916
Wilbourne, Rosa Myers 8/18/1916
Wilburn, Mary (Mrs. C. S.)
6/25/1920
Wilkerson, Emma 1/25/1918
Williams, Mary 3/9/1917
Williams, Mary 3/30/1917

Williams, J. Watts 2/22/1918
Williams, J. Watt 3/15/1918
Williams, Thomas F. 8/30/1918
Williams, Littie 12/27/1918
Williams, Agnes 5/30/1919
Williams, Mr. and Mrs. Charles-
son 6/25/1920
Williams Ruby-brother 6/25/1920
Williams, Mr. and Mrs. W. N.-
daughter 10/29/1920
Williamson, Courtney 10/18/1918
Wilson, Mary Susan 1/9/1920
Winfree, John Bell, Sr. 11/15/1918
Wingfield, Vashi (Mrs. Robert)
12/21/1917
Wolridge, Meriam 2/20/1920
Worsham, Mrs. Pless 1/10/1919
Wright, Doyal 1/31/1919
Young, "Aunt" Dinah 3/29/1918
Younger, Kate 7/6/1917
Trent   10/17/1919
Mail carrier report on death of
family 4/2/1920
Memory of Father-no name
9/17/1920